New Directions for Student Leadership

Susan R. Komives
EDITOR-IN-CHIEF

Kathy L. Guthrie
ASSOCIATE EDITOR

Student Leadership Development Through Recreation and Athletics

Donald A. Stenta
Cara W. McFadden
EDITORS

NIRSA
Leaders in Collegiate
Recreation

Number 147 • Fall 2015
Jossey-Bass
San Francisco

STUDENT LEADERSHIP DEVELOPMENT THROUGH RECREATION AND ATHLETICS
Donald A. Stenta, Cara W. McFadden (eds.)
New Directions for Student Leadership, No. 147, Fall 2015

Susan R. Komives, Editor-in-Chief
Kathy L. Guthrie, Associate Editor

Microfilm copies of issues and articles are available in 16mm and 35mm, as well as microfiche in 105mm, through University Microfilms Inc., 300 North Zeeb Road, Ann Arbor, MI 48106-1346.

New Directions for Student Leadership is indexed in Academic Search Alumni Edition (EBSCO Publishing), Education Index/Abstracts (EBSCO Publishing), ERA: Educational Research Abstracts Online (T&F), ERIC: Educational Resources Information Center (CSC), MLA International Bibliography (MLA).

NEW DIRECTIONS FOR STUDENT LEADERSHIP (ISSN 2373-3349, electronic ISSN 2373-3357) is part of the Jossey-Bass Higher and Adult Education Series and is published quarterly by Wiley Subscription Services, Inc., A Wiley Company, at Jossey-Bass, One Montgomery Street, Suite 1200, San Francisco, CA 94104-4594. POSTMASTER: Send all address changes to New Directions for Student Leadership, Jossey-Bass, One Montgomery Street, Suite 1200, San Francisco, CA 94104-4594.

SUBSCRIPTIONS for print only: $89.00 for individuals in the U.S./Canada/Mexico; $113.00 international. For institutions, agencies, and libraries, $342.00 U.S.; $382.00 Canada/Mexico; $416.00 international. Electronic only: $89.00 for individuals all regions; $342.00 for institutions all regions. Print and electronic: $98.00 for individuals in the U.S., Canada, and Mexico; $122.00 for individuals for the rest of the world; $411.00 for institutions in the U.S.; $451.00 for institutions in Canada and Mexico; $485.00 for institutions for the rest of the world. Prices subject to change. Refer to the order form that appears at the back of most volumes of this journal.

EDITORIAL CORRESPONDENCE should be sent to the Associate Editor, Kathy L. Guthrie, at kguthrie@fsu.edu.

Cover design: Wiley
Cover Images: © Lava 4 images | Shutterstock

www.josseybass.com

About NIRSA: Leaders in Collegiate Recreation

NIRSA is a leader in higher education and the advocate for the advancement of recreation, sport, and wellness by providing educational and developmental opportunities, generating and sharing knowledge, and promoting networking and growth for our members. Since its founding in 1950, NIRSA membership has grown to comprise nearly 4,500 dedicated professionals, students, and businesses, serving an estimated 8.1 million students.

NIRSA is the premier association of leaders in higher education who transform lives and inspire the development of healthy communities worldwide. Leadership, teamwork, dedication, and respect are among the many skills exercised by inclusive competition, fitness, and recreation. As college and university students develop into future leaders, NIRSA members support their learning and growth by fostering lifelong habits of wellbeing.

CONTENTS

EDITORS' NOTES

The purpose of this *New Directions for Student Leadership* sourcebook is to engage higher education professionals with concrete competencies that will enhance the understanding of how students' leadership capacity is developed in recreation and athletic environments. Developing the leadership capacity of students has become an essential outcome in a variety of settings within the higher education environment over the past decade.

This sourcebook captures frameworks for college student leadership development through the lens of the Social Change Model of Leadership Development (HERI, 1996), the Multi-Institutional Study of Leadership (MLS; Dugan, Kodama, Correia, & Associates, 2013), and the Leadership Identity Development (LID) model (Komives, Longerbeam, Owen, Mainella, & Osteen, 2006). In addition, the book highlights other widely used models including the Relational Leadership Model (Komives, Lucas, & McMahon, 2013), the Leadership Challenge (Kouzes & Posner, 2006), and Strengths-Based Leadership (Rath & Conchie, 2008).

We chose these concepts to illustrate the important foundation they create to assist educators in understanding progressive student leadership development within recreation and athletic environments. Our goal is to have student life and academic affairs professionals appreciate the experiences and opportunities for developing leadership capacity in students through recreation and athletics. There is a need for students, staff, and faculty to understand that there is more to recreation and sport than just the activity itself. We need professionals who have the knowledge and skill sets to nurture the development of leadership capacity of all college students.

The primary audience is higher education professionals in a variety of settings: recreation facilities and programs, athletic administrators, and student life and academic affairs professionals. With a variety of students involved in groups on our campuses, our book provides a great resource for practitioners and educators to enhance their abilities to positively influence the leadership development of students throughout their time at the university.

The introductory chapter defines the Social Change Model of Leadership Development, reviews the Relational Leadership Model, and presents the Leadership Challenge to provide a framework for the remainder of the book. In Chapter 1, as editors, we present frameworks that can be used in recreation and athletic settings. This foundational chapter defines today's recreation and athletics contexts, provides perspectives about how

New Directions for Student Leadership, no. 147, Fall 2015 © 2015 Wiley Periodicals, Inc., A Wiley Company
Published online in Wiley Online Library (wileyonlinelibrary.com) • DOI: 10.1002/yd.20138

engagement in these environments contributes to student learning and positive social change, and explores and applies leadership frameworks in recreation and athletics.

Chapter 2, by Gordon M. Nesbitt and Anthony Grant, describe ways to implement key findings from the Multi-Institutional Study of Leadership (MSL) in collegiate recreation and intercollegiate athletic settings. Lessons from the National Collegiate Athletic Association (NCAA) and the NIRSA: Leaders in Collegiate Recreation Leadership Commission are also shared.

Stacey L. Hall discusses the Leadership Identity Development (LID) model in Chapter 3 and how it is used to identify stages for developing leadership capacity. Further discussion provides professionals with approaches for implementing the model in recreation and athletic settings to create environments that support the development of students' leadership capacity.

Understanding the transition from high school to college for student-athletes is imperative. Joy Gaston Gayles and Ashley R. Baker, authors of Chapter 4, provide insight into the transition from high school to college for student-athletes. Additional discussion expands on student-athlete identity and impacts on identity during the transitional phase.

Chapter 5, by Anthony Weaver and Kathleen Simet, explores student-athlete campus engagement and challenges faced by athletes and how that may impede leadership development. Current approaches related to developing student-athlete leadership capacity are shared.

Cara W. McFadden and Julia Wallace Carr share conceptual and practical explanations for developing leadership capacity of collegiate recreation student employees. Chapter 6 provides a discussion around student development and leadership theories, roles of student employees, and current practice.

Chapter 7, by Amy C. Barnes and James Larcus, expands on the foundational leadership development frameworks and highlights the field of positive psychology. Constructs like hope and optimism, and a strengths-based focus for individual and group development, are explored to optimize the development of student leadership capacity.

Elizabeth A. Speelman and Mark Wagstaff deliver critical perspectives about experiential education and discuss the involvement, motivation, and reflection that students experience during the process of participating in adventure leadership in Chapter 8.

Chapter 9, by Sarah E. Hardin, is the final chapter of the sourcebook, and provides the reader with literature and resources for conducting leadership assessment in collegiate recreation and athletics, highlighting the critical nature of assessment in developing undergraduate student leadership capacity.

We hope you enjoy the thoughts and reflections of these leadership educators and practitioners. Our hope is to empower the reader with a different way of thinking about student leadership development in collegiate

NEW DIRECTIONS FOR STUDENT LEADERSHIP • DOI: 10.1002/yd

recreation and intercollegiate athletic environments. In addition, we hope the ideas shared are relevant to your own work in developing student leadership capacity. For all readers, this sourcebook is a reminder that leadership learning occurs in unique settings throughout our colleges and universities. Here is one guided source that illustrates how we might achieve this work in collegiate recreation and athletic settings.

Donald A. Stenta
Cara W. McFadden
Editors

References

Dugan, J. P., Kodama, C., Correia, B., & Associates (2013). *Multi-Institutional Study of Leadership insight report: Leadership program delivery*. College Park, MD: National Clearinghouse for Leadership Programs.

Higher Education Research Institute [HERI]. (1996). *A social change model of leadership development: Guidebook version III*. College Park, MD: National Clearinghouse for Leadership Programs.

Komives, S. R., Longerbeam, S. D., Owen, J. E., Mainella, F. C., & Osteen, L. (2006). A leadership identity development model: Applications from a grounded theory. *Journal of College Student Development*, 47, 401–420.

Komives, S. R., Lucas, N., & McMahon, T. R. (2013). *Exploring leadership: For college students who want to make a difference* (3rd ed.). San Francisco, CA: Jossey-Bass.

Kouzes, J. M., & Posner, B. Z. (2006). *Leadership challenge: How to make extraordinary things happen in organizations*. San Francisco, CA: Jossey-Bass.

Rath, T., & Conchie, B. (2008). *Strengths-based leadership*. New York, NY: Gallup Press.

DONALD A. STENTA *has been at the Ohio State University for nearly 25 years in higher education and student affairs roles. He currently serves as the director of Student Life Recreational Sports and as a lecturer with the John Glenn College of Public Affairs, where he teaches classes in leadership and public policy. Stenta has been a long-time member of ACPA—College Student Educators International and currently serves on the board of directors for NIRSA: Leaders in Collegiate Recreation.*

CARA W. MCFADDEN *has 15 combined years of experience in collegiate recreation and higher education. She is an assistant professor in sport and event management within the School of Communications at Elon University. McFadden has been a long-time member of NIRSA: Leaders in Collegiate Recreation and has served as a member of the Assembly, cochair for the Leadership Commission, and faculty for the NIRSA School of Collegiate Recreation.*

NEW DIRECTIONS FOR STUDENT LEADERSHIP • DOI: 10.1002/yd

1

Collegiate recreation and intercollegiate athletics have an impact on individual, group, and community development of students who are participants, employees, and athletes and learn leadership within these environments. This chapter explores and applies leadership frameworks in recreation and athletics.

Connecting Collegiate Recreation and Athletics to Leadership

Cara W. McFadden, Donald A. Stenta

Recreation and athletics programs are developmentally powerful environments holistically engaging students in challenging situations. These focused experiences provide opportunities for intentional development of effective individual and team leadership that supports institutional learning goals. Developmentally based programs and interventions emerge when higher education professionals proactively design a leadership development curriculum that meets students where they are and takes them to new stages that facilitate their growth and development. This chapter discusses a variety of leadership models and perspectives that professionals could choose to infuse in their collegiate recreation and athletic environments for the purpose of developing student leadership capacity.

Collegiate recreation programs emerged following the lead of the Ohio State University and the University of Michigan. Both institutions created intramural programs in 1913, spawning the structure for recreation and intramural programs today. Michigan then opened the nation's first intramural sports building in 1928 and more universities followed suit. In 1950, due to the lack of integrated sport activity, the National Intramural Association (NIA) was founded at Dillard University. The NIA was designed to facilitate intramural activities for students of color at predominantly White institutions and students enrolled at historically Black colleges and universities. The NIA evolved to become NIRSA, initially called the National Intramural and Recreational Sports Association, but now known as NIRSA: Leaders in Collegiate Recreation (NIRSA, n.d.). Although most recreation programs were founded as an aspect of a college or university athletic department, the vast majority of recreation programs report through a student

```
```

affairs/life unit today. Other reporting lines include athletic departments, academic colleges/schools, or business/auxiliary units. Collegiate recreation programs today offer a wide range of activities in various facility types and styles. Most collegiate recreation departments include adaptive or inclusive programs, adventure/outdoor pursuits activities, aquatics, camps and community programs, competitive sports (intramural and sport clubs), group exercise or fitness programs, instructional and safety lessons, and personal training. Departments also include administrative support areas like advancement, assessment, business sponsorship, facilities management and development, marketing and creative services, membership sales and services, and student and staff training and development.

Intercollegiate athletics have been a focus on college and university campuses since the mid-1840s, with structures like local and national governing bodies developing over 60 years later (Smith, 2009). The National Collegiate Athletic Association (NCAA) was founded in 1906 and serves as the lead entity in shaping and developing national policy for athletics. Athletic departments on college and university campuses are led by an administrator typically called an athletic director, and are very complex organizations that include associate or assistant athletic directors (who typically serve as administrators for a large number of sports and supervise the coaching staff) and staff who are focused in business services, communications, facility development, fundraising and development, human resources, nutrition and high performance training, student-athlete development and academic support, and ticketing and customer service.

Collegiate recreation and intercollegiate athletic environments vary based on institutional size, organizational structures, societal expectations, and the university mission. Understanding the complexity of leadership development in these environments is imperative, as "successful collegiate leadership programs are embedded in and aligned with the following four contextual layers: higher education's purpose, institutional mission, administrative support, and collaborative environment. Each of these layers contributes to or detracts from desired student learning outcomes" (Osteen & Coburn, 2012, p. 5).

Although recreation and athletics have seemingly similar goals in developing students and supporting athletes and physical activity, the efforts that exist on college campus today are not typically aligned. There is great potential, however, in exploring leadership development in the context of physical activity, sport, and recreation.

Rapid local and global change requires institutions of higher education to increase leadership development programs within their select university environment. Roberts (2007) identifies leadership development as a priority and expresses that leadership learning is the primary purpose of higher education. Collegiate recreation and intercollegiate athletic programs typically engage in participant, employee, and athletic training development where the learning is focused on skill development based on the work of the employee or the skill level of the athlete's performance.

This lack of clarity is evident in the collegiate recreation and intercollegiate athletics literature. Although uses of conceptual models are limited, this does not mean that leadership perspectives are not being used. We sought to identify current efforts and share these so more professionals in collegiate recreation and intercollegiate athletic environments will have resources to guide their practice. This chapter explores student leadership development through the use of the Social Change Model of Leadership Development (SCM; HERI, 1996; Komives & Wagner, 2009) as a foundation for developing leadership capacity as well as comparing the model to the Relational Leadership Model (RLM; Komives, Lucas, & McMahon, 2013) and the Leadership Challenge (Kouzes & Posner, 2006).

Resources to Support Practitioners

Reviewing the literature related to leadership development can be overwhelming to professionals who may not have the time to dedicate to the study of leadership. There are resources available to practitioners, for example, *The Handbook for Student Leadership Development* (Komives, Dugan, Owen, Slack, & Wagner, 2011) and *The Student Leadership Competencies Guidebook* (Seemiller, 2013). Both provide resources for practitioners and express the responsibility for practitioners to apply critical thought processes to leadership education and development.

The National Clearinghouse for Leadership Programs (NCLP) publication titled *Collegiate Recreational Sports and Student Leadership Development* (Blumenthal, 2010) includes an issue with emphasis on leadership through intercollegiate, intramural, and recreational athletics. The issue highlights the role of collegiate recreation leadership development, the need for athletic leadership development, and intramural sports captains' leadership capacity, and it provides updates regarding sport and leadership development (Blumenthal, 2010).

Leadership Development Models

Selecting a model or perspective provides support for applying theory to practice.

> Too often practitioners think only of programming when they ponder ways to use theory in practice. While programming is important, theory is also extremely helpful when advising or counseling students, advising student organizations, designing classroom instruction and training initiatives, and formulating policy. (Evans, Forney, Guido, Patton, & Renn, 2010, p. 369)

Intentionally using one of the leadership perspectives mentioned throughout this issue provides a foundation for an integrated leadership approach

NEW DIRECTIONS FOR STUDENT LEADERSHIP • DOI: 10.1002/yd

that can be applied in the collegiate recreation or athletics environment to enhance the development of student leadership capacity.

Social Change Model as a Foundation.   Over 20 years ago, the Social Change Model of Leadership Development (SCM) was developed by leadership educators through a grant from the Dwight D. Eisenhower Leadership Development Program of the U.S. Department of Education. University educators use the SCM to describe the values that are necessary for leaders to develop as an individual, within a group, or as part of a community (HERI, 1996; Komives & Wagner, 2009). A leadership development model like this is a useful tool to define concepts that can be applied in leadership programs and activities. The SCM approaches leadership as "a purposeful, collaborative, values-based process that results in positive social change" (Komives & Wagner, 2009, p. xii).

Overall, the model's focus is to advocate for social responsibility and the common good. To accomplish this, the model is composed of seven core values that interact with individual, group, and community stages, with the goal being to engage others in collaborative work (Dugan, 2006). (See Table 1.1.)

An eighth value, focused on change, brings together all seven values to affect change (see Figure 1.1). Although each set of values influences the others as represented in the arrows, research shows that leadership development occurs with the individual first, then in the group context, which in turns inform community development and change (Dugan, Bohle, Woelker, & Cooney, 2014).

Implementing this model is a challenge because university environments are complex and sometimes difficult to navigate. For example, students at community colleges and institutions with a large commuter base tend to have significant diversity of student enrollment type, including international students, first-generation students, and adult students, who, along with traditional aged college students, bring diverse experiences into the university environment. Students come to the university with a complexity of multiple identities and grow and change during their time at the institution.

The use of models such as the SCM and other leadership perspectives that follow provide resources for practitioners to better understand these complexities. These models provide faculty, staff, and students with tools to create and support initiatives in and out of the classroom that enhance the development of students' leadership capacity.

Relational Leadership Model.   The Relational Leadership Model (RLM) is a model that can be considered in the collegiate recreation or intercollegiate athletics context. This model, developed by Susan Komives, Nance Lucas, and Tim McMahon (2013), essentially reframes leadership as a "relational and ethical process of people together attempting to accomplish positive change" (Komives, Lucas, & McMahon, 2007, p. 14). The RLM emphasizes the elements of being purposeful, inclusive, empowering,

Table 1.1   The Critical Values of the Social Change Model

Individual Values

Consciousness of Self	Being aware of the beliefs, values, attitudes, and emotions that motivate you to take action. Being mindful or aware of your current emotional state, behavior, and perceptual lenses.
Congruence	Acting in ways that are consistent with your values and beliefs. Thinking, feeling, and behaving with consistency, genuineness, authenticity, and honesty toward others.
Commitment	Having significant investment in an idea or person, both in terms of intensity and duration. Having the energy to serve the group and its goals. Commitment originates from within, but others can create an environment that supports an individual's passions.

Group Values

Collaboration	Working with others in a common effort, sharing responsibility, authority, and accountability. Multiplying group effectiveness by capitalizing on various perspectives and talents and on the power of diversity to generate creative solutions and actions.
Common Purpose	Having shared aims and values. Involving others in building a group's vision and purpose.
Controversy With Civility	Recognizing the fundamental realities of any creative effort: (1) that differences in viewpoint are inevitable, and (2) that such differences must be aired openly but with civility.

Community Values

Citizenship	Believing in a process whereby an individual or a group becomes responsibly connected to the community and society through some activity. Recognizing that members of communities are not independent but interdependent. Recognizing individuals and groups have responsibility for the welfare of others.

Because it is a key assumption of the SCM that the ultimate goal of leadership is positive social change, "change" is considered to be at the "hub" of the SCM.

Change	Believing in the importance of making a better world and a better society for oneself and others. Believing that individuals, groups, and communities have the ability to work together to make that change.

Adapted from Higher Education Institute, 1996, p. 21; Tyree, 1998, p. 176; and Astin, 1996, pp. 6–7. Originally published in W. Wagner (2007). The social change model of leadership: A brief overview. *Concepts & Connections, 15*(1), 9.

Figure 1.1.   The Social Change Model of Leadership Development

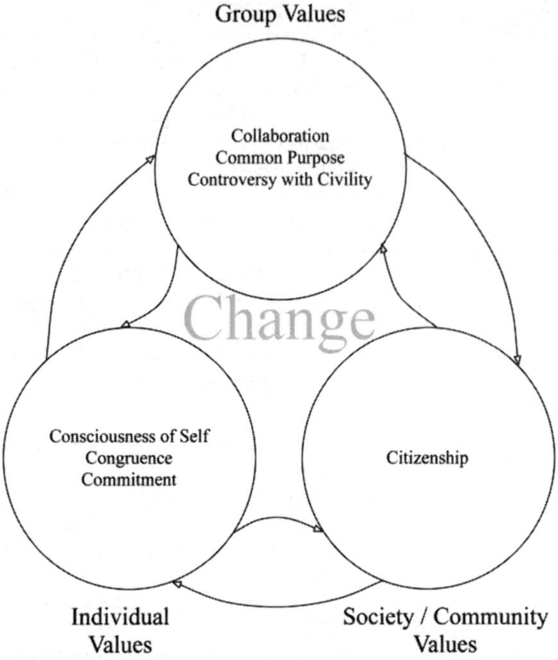

Adapted from *A social change model of leadership development* (3rd ed., p. 20) by Higher Education Research Institute [HERI]. Copyright © 1996, National Clearinghouse for Leadership Programs. Reprinted with permission of the National Clearinghouse for Leadership Programs.

ethical, and process oriented. Because the model is considered to be an aspirational model (Haber, 2008), leaders and organizations can consistently apply aspects of the model in a continuing quest for improvement and excellence. The most important aspect of the model is the focus on values and relationships that emerge from a values-driven approach to leadership.

This definition and the elements of the model intentionally bring together people who are working with one another toward a common journey. But it is the inclusion of three key aspects that serves as a way to think differently about leadership in recreation or athletics contexts: relationships, ethics, and change.

These recreation or athletic contexts almost always celebrate wins in terms of one team dominating another team for a championship or for a series of accomplishments where there are winners and losers. The competitive environment appears only to link to traditional models of leadership, and coaches, athletes, administrators, and fans alike might have a narrow view of what leadership means in these contexts. So it might seem inconsistent to enter into an exploration about leadership development with a focus on relationships. But there is plenty of room to discuss a focus on relationships in competitive and team environments. If a more relational environment could be developed, and if competitive sport also included regular reflections about the relational process of people coming together, professionals in these areas could make significant differences in developing students as leaders. This can happen while also honoring the competitive process, respecting talent and effort, and providing challenges for personal and group mastery and excellence.

Programs that operate from a "win at all costs" mentality can struggle in infusing ethical behavior for student-athletes and participants in collegiate recreation programs. Athletes and fans alike can benefit from links to ethical standards in competitions. Sportsmanship programs across the country seek to encourage deep fan commitment and engagement, while at the same time putting the athletic challenge into perspective: that the athletes are students first, and the sport offering can lead to productive connections to community pride that should result in contributions to the common good (Reid, 2010). However, these connections are not made easily and without interventions. High school and college recreation and athletic administrators ought to be structuring sportsmanship activities that can lead to enhancing and improving the common good.

In addition, ethical behaviors can be discussed in student staff training programs, outdoor adventure settings, or athlete development meetings, but what about actively discussing these issues in competitive environments? How often does this happen? When looking at continuing challenges with NCAA infractions or with university leadership challenges, one wonders how young people can find role models to lead the path regarding these behaviors. This role modeling needs to occur in sharp and positive ways, with coaches and staff structuring more focused behaviors for athletes. Lack of positive role modeling could lead older students to develop poor habits and traditions that lead to hazing and unethical and/or illegal practices.

Although a focus on relationships and on ethical processes is an important aspect of the RLM, it is perhaps the intentional connection to "positive change" that sets the stage for taking leadership concepts to the next level. Positive change in recreation and sports can exist when athletes are approached with a full development plan, where needs inside and outside of the classroom and on and off of play venues are honored. Positive change in recreation and sports can occur when traditional methods of leading groups are used so that coaches can direct plays and practice schedules, but that team captains can also be engaged so that peer involvement can facilitate learning. Positive change in recreation and sports can occur when fans, staff, and administrators understand the impact that can be made in a community when a proper focus is placed on health and well-being, community pride and engagement, and academic achievements and graduation rates (Komives et al., 2013). Athletes who shun responsibilities to serve as role models, who do not think of their place in their communities,

Table 1.2   Relational Leadership Model Applied to
Recreation and Athletics

RLM Element	Application to Recreation and Athletics
Purposeful	Intentionally develop all athletes, participants, and student employees into leaders; create intentional training programs; align theory and published research findings to program development
Inclusive	Encourage diverse viewpoints; teach and train about managing conflicts in a positive manner; facilitate challenge by choice principles in adventure programming; develop curriculum for leading sociocultural conversations
Empowering	Seek to understand individual differences; provide information needed for the full participation of individuals; expect upper-class students to be role models; facilitate mentorship programming
Ethical	Apply rules of play consistently; practice positive sportsmanship; do not cheat; credit individuals with their useful ideas and contributions; uphold high personal ethical standards; uphold standards and rules
Process oriented	Build community; debrief events and activities; conduct postgame/postexperience reflection activities and opportunities; give all participants opportunities for involvement and feedback; offer structured feedback sessions

and who lack a structured vision for giving back to their communities miss incredibly important opportunities to grow a generation of interested, engaged, and committed citizens. This potential positive change has been absent for too long and can be developed with high school and college students.

Students who are involved in the leadership process must truly understand themselves before they can effectively work with others to influence change within their communities (e.g., collegiate recreation, athletics, or the university as a whole). This occurs by knowing (knowledgeable), being (aware of self and others), and doing (to act). Overall, the goal must be purposeful and the student must have a commitment to the activity (Komives et al., 2013). Table 1.2 illustrates how elements of the model apply in recreation and athletics settings.

Leadership Challenge.   In the late 1980s, Jim Kouzes and Barry Posner wished to understand what leadership behaviors the best leaders engaged in during their regular work. Through a series of surveys and focus groups, hundreds of tasks and observable practices were revealed and were grouped into five leadership "practices." The five practices include challenging the process, inspiring a shared vision, modeling the way, enabling others to act, and encouraging the heart (Kouzes & Posner, 1987).

NEW DIRECTIONS FOR STUDENT LEADERSHIP • DOI: 10.1002/yd

Table 1.3   The Five Practices and Ten Commitments of Leadership

Practice	Commitment
Model the Way	1. Clarify values by finding your voice and affirming shared ideals.
	2. Set the example by aligning actions with shared values.
Inspire a Shared Vision	3. Envision the future by imagining exciting and ennobling possibilities.
	4. Enlist others in a common vision by appealing to shared aspirations.
Challenge the Process	5. Search for opportunities by seizing the initiative and by looking outward for innovative ways to improve.
	6. Experiment and take risks by constantly generating small wins and learning from experience.
Enable Others to Act	7. Foster collaboration by building trust and facilitating relationships.
	8. Strengthen others by increasing self-determination and developing competence.
Encourage the Heart	9. Recognize contributions by showing appreciation for individual excellence.
	10. Celebrate the values and victories by creating a spirit of community.

Originally published in J. M. Kouzes & B. Z. Posner (2006), *Leadership challenge: How to make extraordinary things happen in organizations* (4th ed.). San Francisco, CA: Jossey-Bass.

An assessment called the Leadership Practices Inventory (Kouzes & Posner, 1987) was developed to provide feedback about leadership styles. This assessment grew from research with managers in private sector organizations, whereas follow-up studies were conducted with educational institutions including student organizations through a student version of the Leadership Practices Inventory (Kouzes & Posner, 2006).

The most significant development with this framework is the inclusive tone of the five leadership practices. Prior leadership assessments like the Strategic Leadership Style Instrument (Reagan, 1993) offered feedback across eight different leadership styles, where at least three were considered negative leadership styles. The Leadership Challenge (see Table 1.3) encourages leaders to think about how to incorporate all five practices in their experiences and posits that all five practices should be represented for organizational success. The outcome of this approach is a movement toward more positive, inclusive, and asset-based considerations about one's leadership style. The more positive tone in this model, where all five practices contribute equally and in tandem with one another, can dispel a "this is right; that is wrong" approach in understanding leadership. The inclusive nature of this model allows leaders with preferences for different practices to prosper in equal ways.

Environment Changes

With the constant interconnections between students, institutions, and society, it is imperative that as advocates for fostering student leadership capacity we critically think about college students and their development within campus learning environments. The developmental ecology model developed by Renn and Arnold (2003) describes the interactions students have with the campus environment and their peers. The researchers suggest that the ecology model could be useful for creating intentional interventions to promote the development of college students (Renn & Arnold, 2003). Studying recreation and athletic environments could assist in better applying this understanding.

Recreation. The mission statement of collegiate recreation departments drives the purpose and goals for the organization. Typically these settings are influenced by the university mission and goals set to support lifelong learning and educational experiences. Departments are multifaceted in regard to the components (e.g., facilities, peers, sport club activity, professional staff, customers) that contribute to the environment. The placement of these departments within the university also guides the mission; some departments are found in the division of student affairs or athletics. One of the most prevalent factors that describe the purpose of collegiate recreation on most campuses is a holistic approach, where there is focus on physical, mental, and emotional development (Franklin & Hardin, 2008).

Athletics. There are over 460,000 intercollegiate student-athletes who compete in 23 sports every year. In addition, eight out of ten student-athletes will obtain a bachelor's degree and more than 30 percent will earn a postgraduate degree (NCAA, n.d.). The intercollegiate athletic environment is composed of physical (athletic facilities, university facilities), social (housing, class group projects, family members, teammates), and cognitive experiences (in and out of class). Most of the literature surrounding intercollegiate athletics highlights the intense time commitment student-athletes contribute to being an athlete and how it affects their academic success (Miller & Kerr, 2003, Nite, 2012). Intercollegiate athletes are often marked as "at-risk" students especially during the first-year experience when students are transitioning from high school to college (Wilson & Pritchard, 2005). In Chapter 4, there is further discussion focused specifically on the transition of the student-athlete from high school to college.

Environmental scans in collegiate recreation and intercollegiate athletics can offer proper perspective about creating institutional priorities, professional association goals, and staff and student development activities. For over a century, most collegiate recreation programs have operated inwardly in developing recreation programming that responds to student needs and has been driven by participant satisfaction surveys and feedback. Facilities have expanded in order to support additional program offerings. Once based on intuition for the past 20 years or so, assessment activities have been grounded in empirical research and are now aligned to a student learning agenda. This needs to continue. Collegiate recreation programs must develop a consolidated agenda that examines how participation in recreation activities can have a positive impact on student academic performance and other learning and developmental outcomes. Measurement should be in line with how academic partners prioritize the student learning agenda. If a college or university is focused on links to student academic success by measuring grade point averages (GPAs), then the collegiate recreation program and athletic accomplishment must also measure engagement and links to student GPAs.

Balance of Challenge and Support.   Finding the right balance between challenge and support for students' leadership development in these environments is vital. Sanford (1966) suggests students must be prepared and in a state of readiness before challenge is introduced. Students are ready based on internal maturation or environmental factors. Once the student is ready, challenge can be introduced; however, the student can tolerate the challenge based on the amount of support that is available (Evans et al., 2010). If there is not the right balance between challenge and support, the opportunity to develop leadership capacity could be lost.

Using the Social Change Model and other perspectives in comparison can assist in creating a supportive environment with intentional planning for a productive setting where students develop their leadership capacity in a productive manner. Creating this balance is important because students find themselves at differing stages within their development during their time in college.

Students can perceive their world and interpret experiences in two different ways, "(1) reinterpret the experience in ways that allow them to maintain their current lens or (2) change to a new lens that better explains the new experience," (Wagner, 2011, p. 86). As students progress through the second way of interpreting their world, Wagner (2011) states that students experience a period of disequilibrium due to the transition between developmental stages. This idea of disequilibrium lends students to change their way of thinking and is referred to as *readiness*. Students thrive in environments and exhibit readiness when there are meaningful levels of challenge and support (Wagner, 2011).

Collegiate recreation and athletic environments that create such a balance provide students with the opportunity to manage their current stage of development with support and progress to the next stage of development by receiving accurate levels of challenge. For example, intramural officials receive significant amounts of training and support during official's development programs. They are equipped with rulebooks, policy details, historical perspective, hand motions and style guidelines, and a uniform to do their jobs. However, during an athletic contest, they—and they alone—must blow the whistle, stop play, and make the call.

Conclusion

Understanding the practical use of leadership development frameworks is key for the success of building college student leadership capacity. Dugan and Komives (2010) suggest there is a critical juncture between research and practice that embrace theory and conceptual frameworks regarding the development of student leadership capacity that is grounded in social responsibility.

Connecting collegiate recreation and athletics to the models or perspectives explained in this chapter are complex and multifaceted. With the varying environments in recreation and athletics, there are myriad opportunities to develop student leaders by means of applying leadership developmental models. The use of a framework or model will be dependent upon the environment and context it is being used. Our hopes are that the following chapters provide deeper understanding and examples of how to integrate one or multiple frameworks in a variety of collegiate recreation and athletic environments. Professional staff serve as advisors, mentors, and supervisors, so these interactions with students are integral in the development and learning of student leadership capacity. Staff should use the suggested models and frameworks to form the leadership capacity of participants, student-athletes, and students employed in these unique environments.

References

Blumenthal, K. J. (2010). Collegiate recreational sports and student leadership development. *Concepts & Connections: Leadership Through Intercollegiate, Intramural, and Recreational Athletics, 17*(1), 1–5.

Dugan, J. P. (2006). Explorations using the social change model: Leadership development among college men and women. *Journal of College Student Development, 47,* 217–225.

Dugan, J. P., & Komives, S. R. (2010). Influence on college students' capacities for socially responsible leadership. *Journal of College Student Development, 51,* 525–549.

Dugan, J. P., Bohle, C. W., Woelker, L. R., & Cooney, M. A. (2014). The role of social perspective-taking in developing students' leadership capacities. *Journal of Student Affairs Research and Practice, 51*(1), 1–15.

Evans, N. J., Forney, D. S., Guido, F. M., Patton, L. D., & Renn, K. A. (2010). *Student development in college: Theory, research, and practice* (2nd ed.). San Francisco, CA: Jossey-Bass.

Franklin, D. S., & Hardin, S. E. (2008). Philosophical and theoretical foundations of campus recreation: Crossroads of theory. In National Intramural-Recreational Sports Association [NIRSA], *Campus recreation: Essentials for the professional* (pp. 3–20). Champaign, IL: Human Kinetics.

Haber, P. (2008). Leadership models for college students [Power Point slides]. Retrieved from https://nclp.umd.edu/leadership_educators_institute/haber-_lei_pre-institute-_leadership_models_for_college_students.ppt

Higher Education Research Institute [HERI]. (1996). *A social change model of leadership development: Guidebook version III.* College Park, MD: National Clearinghouse for Leadership Programs.

Komives, S. R., & Wagner, W. (Eds). (2009). *Leadership for a better world: Understanding the social change model of leadership development.* San Francisco, CA: Jossey-Bass.

Komives, S. R., Dugan, J. P., Owen, J. E., Slack, C., & Wagner, W. (2011). *The handbook for student leadership development.* San Francisco, CA: Jossey-Bass.

Komives, S. R., Lucas, N., & McMahon, T. R. (2007). *Exploring leadership: For college students who want to make a difference* (2nd ed.). San Francisco, CA: Jossey-Bass.

Komives, S. R., Lucas, N., & McMahon, T. R. (2013). *Exploring leadership: For college students who want to make a difference* (3rd ed.). San Francisco, CA: Jossey-Bass.

Kouzes, J. M., & Posner, B. Z. (1987). *Leadership challenge: How to make extraordinary things happen in organizations* (1st ed.). San Francisco, CA: Jossey-Bass.

Kouzes, J. M., & Posner, B. Z. (2006). *Leadership challenge: How to make extraordinary things happen in organizations* (4th ed.). San Francisco, CA: Jossey-Bass.

Miller, P. S., & Kerr, G. A. (2003). Role of experimentation of intercollegiate student athletes. *Sport Psychologist, 17,* 196–219.

NCAA. (n.d.). *Student-athletes.* Retrieved from http://www.ncaa.org/student-athletes

NIRSA: Leaders in Collegiate Recreation. (n.d.) *NIRSA history.* Retrieved from http://nirsa.net/nirsa/about/history/

Nite, C. (2012). Challenges for supporting student-athlete development: Perspectives from an NCAA Division II Athletic Department. *Journal of Issues in Intercollegiate Athletics, 5,* 1–14.

Osteen, L., & Coburn, M. B. (2012). Considering context: Developing students' leadership capacity. In K. L. Guthrie & L. Osteen (Eds.), *New Directions for Student Services: No. 140. Developing student's leadership capacity* (pp. 5–15). San Francisco, CA: Jossey-Bass.

Reagan, G. (1993). Strategic leadership style instrument. In W. E. Pfeiffer (Ed.), *The 1993 annual: Developing human resources* (pp. 161–165). San Francisco, CA: Jossey-Bass.

Reid, H. L. (2010). Leadership and sport. In R. A. Couto (Ed.), *Political and civic leadership: A reference handbook* (pp. 1034–1039). Thousand Oaks, CA: Sage.

Renn, K. A., & Arnold, K. D. (2003). Reconceptualizing research on peer culture. *Journal of Higher Education, 74,* 261–291.

Roberts, D. C. (2007). *Deeper learning in leadership: Helping college students find the potential within.* San Francisco, CA: John Wiley & Sons.

Sanford, N. (1966). *Self and society.* New York, NY: Atherton Press.

Seemiller, C. (2013). *The student leadership competencies guidebook: Designing intentional leadership and learning development.* San Francisco, CA: Jossey-Bass.

Smith, R. K. (2009). *A brief history of the National Collegiate Athletic Association's role in regulating intercollegiate athletics,* 11 Marq. Sports L. Rev. 9 Retrieved from http://scholarship.law.marquette.edu/sportslaw/vol11/iss1/5

Wagner, W. (2007). The social change model of leadership: A brief overview. *Concepts & Connections, 15*(1), 8–9.

Wagner, W. (2011). Considerations of student development in leadership. In S. R. Komives, J. P. Dugan, J. E. Owen, C. Slack, & W. Wagner (Eds.), *The handbook for student leadership development* (pp. 85–107). San Francisco, CA: Jossey-Bass.

Wilson, G., & Pritchard, M. (2005). Comparing sources of stress in college student athletes and non-athletes. *Athletic Insight: The Online Journal of Sport Psychology, 7,* 1–8.

Cara W. McFadden is an assistant professor in Sport and Event Management in the School of Communications at Elon University.

Donald A. Stenta is the director of student life recreational sports and a lecturer with the John Glenn College of Public Affairs at the Ohio State University.

New Directions for Student Leadership • DOI: 10.1002/yd

2

This chapter describes ways to implement key findings of the Multi-Institutional Study of Leadership in collegiate recreation and athletic programs. Lessons from NCAA and the NIRSA Leadership Commission are also presented.

Applying the Multi-Institutional Study of Leadership Findings to Collegiate Recreation and Athletics

Gordon M. Nesbitt, Anthony Grant

The Multi-Institutional Study of Leadership (MSL), published by Dugan, Kodama, Correia, and Associates (2013) released powerful findings for implementing college leadership programs. "The Multi-Institutional Study of Leadership (MSL) is an annual, international survey of leadership development among college students" (Komives, Dugan, Owen, Slack, Wagner, & Associates, 2011, p. 197) that is grounded in the Social Change Model of Leadership Development discussed in Chapter 1. In the early years of the MSL study, Dugan and Komives (2007) framed leadership development for college students by understanding four trends: an expansion of curricular and cocurricular programs, a focus on theoretical and conceptual models, a professionalization in leadership education, and more intentional leadership research. From this research, Dugan et al. (2013) developed 10 recommendations to enrich campus leadership programs. Of the 10 recommendations, 4 are considered high-impact practices. This chapter links these four high-impact practices to a collegiate recreation and athletics setting. The chapter also articulates the work of the NIRSA: Leaders in Collegiate Recreation Leadership Commission and its impact on the collegiate recreation and student affairs profession.

Multi-Institutional Study of Leadership (MSL)

The MSL is based on the Socially Responsible Leadership Scale measuring the Social Change Model of Leadership (SCM) and was developed by Tracy Tyree (1998). The MSL measures the eight values from the SCM discussed in Chapter 1, such as collaboration, controversy with civility, and

New Directions for Student Leadership, no. 147, Fall 2015 © 2015 Wiley Periodicals, Inc., A Wiley Company
Published online in Wiley Online Library (wileyonlinelibrary.com) • DOI: 10.1002/yd.20140

other group dimensions, that are critical in developing student leadership capacity based on how students understand themselves and how students understand difference (such as culture, gender, race, ethnicity). The MSL also assesses a broader range of leadership outcomes and the experiences that influence students. From these data, Dugan, Torrez, and Turman (2014) recently published the *Leadership in Intramurals and Sport Clubs: Examining Influences to Enhance Educational Impact.*

These efforts and the collective work of MSL are a result of the shared commitment and investment made by leadership educators across the world. To date, the administrators of the MSL have collected data from over 250 colleges and universities in Canada, Jamaica, Mexico, and the United States that include over 300,000 diverse participants. Various components of the MSL have also been used in China, Colombia, Italy, Japan, Kenya, Lithuania, and Turkey (Dugan et al., 2014).

The MSL generated evidence that the following high-impact practices were strongly associated with gains in leadership development:

- Sociocultural conversations with peers
- Mentoring relationships
- Community service
- Memberships in off-campus organizations (Dugan et al., 2013)

In addition, the study found that developmental readiness and sequencing of leadership development programs is important to maximize participant learning, which will be addressed in other chapters.

Sociocultural Conversations With Peers. The MSL found that "Socio-cultural conversations with peers are the single strongest predictor of socially responsible leadership capacity for students across demographic groups" (Dugan et al., 2013, p. 9). The report indicates that sociocultural conversations "consist of formal and informal dialogues with peers about differences (i.e., topics which elicit a wide range of perspectives) as well as interactions across differences (e.g., with people who have different backgrounds and beliefs than oneself)" (Dugan et al., 2013, p. 9). Because the authors have identified these conversations as the strongest predictor of socially responsible leadership, it is important to explore how these conversations affect students and how to encourage these conversations to take place.

Some of the influences of sociocultural conversations are identified by Baraja-Rohan (1997):

> Approaching conversation from a cross-cultural perspective gives students an opportunity to explore their own cultural identity and explain to some degree why they operate the way they do. It also shows respect for students' cultural entity and enables second language learners to be valued for their differences. (p. 77)

Involvement in conversations that involve different backgrounds allows students to confront their own, often deeply held, assumptions and creates the possibility of learning about other ways of thinking. Edvalson (2013) goes further and states:

> When students from various races interact on college campuses in the United States, they bring their experiences with and perceptions of the other race to the conversation. These experiences and perceptions influence the way they engage in dialogues with peers. These varying and often competing ideas about and perspectives on race inform the way they make meaning of race and their role in systemic oppression. (p. 93)

Too often, college students drift toward other students who look and think like them. Participation in discussions with students of other races and other dimensions of difference can provide new perceptions about social issues like race, inequality, homelessness, poverty, hazing, sexual violence, or politics.

Komives, Lucas, and McMahon (2013) point out the importance of these conversations to leadership development when they indicate that "effective leaders need to develop an appreciation for multiculturalism to build inclusiveness, collaboration, and common purposes" (p. 196). Leaders need to possess the ability to empathize with others to engender trust. Appreciation for diversity will help student leaders develop the ability to empathize. Building inclusiveness is important to the leadership role, and the Relational Leadership Model (Komives et al., 2013) identifies the following building blocks of inclusiveness:

- Know yourself and others; engage yourself in learning new information as you develop the competencies required in your role (knowledge)
- Be open to difference and value other perspectives (attitudes)
- Practice listening skills, coalition building, interpersonal skills, and effective civil discourse (skills). (p. 97)

Engaging in conversations with others allows participants to develop these building blocks and incorporate them into their overall leadership capacity.

Sociocultural discussions can occur in formal, semiformal, or informal settings. In the collegiate recreation settings, formal conversations should be included in staff training programs, staff meetings, and club sports officer-training sessions. Having a diverse staff allows for sensitive issues to be discussed and creates a setting for all staff or officers to dispel assumptions and stereotypes. Confidentiality and trust must be established before these conversations will be productive. Building partnerships with the staff from departments whose purpose is social equity and bringing them to training meetings initiates the process of communication between different groups.

Campus-wide or departmental leadership development training programs are another area where both collegiate recreation and intercollegiate athletics encourage students to engage in sociocultural conversations. Most leadership development programs have a diversity component that should create an atmosphere for open conversations. Several websites offer examples of programs.

- *Center for Leadership at Elon University*: http://www.elon.edu/e-web/students/leadership/default.xhtml (Elon University, n.d.)
- *Leadership Development at Ithaca College*: http://www.ithaca.edu/sacl/osema/leadership/ (Ithaca College, n.d.)
- *Leadership Education Advancement Project (LEAP) at Lycoming College*: http://www.lycoming.edu/studentPrograms/leap.aspx (Lycoming College, n.d.)

Collaboration with other campus departments that already have opportunities for diversity education and sociocultural conversations can help share the effort involved. If there are no leadership development programs offered through the student affairs division, collegiate recreation and intercollegiate athletics staff are able to take the lead and start programs to develop student leadership capacity.

Including information in captains' meetings is an example of a semiformal opportunity for sociocultural discussions. Discussion about cultural and racial differences is often included in captains' meetings where team captains are learning the components of sportsmanship. Student-athletes should also hear about these issues during team meetings and training sessions. Sportsmanship may have different meanings to different groups, and it is important to understand that some actions might be viewed as disrespectful to one group and gamesmanship to another. All participants need to understand norms of what will and what will not be tolerated during sporting activities and the consequences of actions that will not be tolerated. Engaging student-athletes in conversations of what is not allowed and why it is not allowed may open the door to meaningful dialogue on differences.

Informal opportunities for conversations in collegiate recreation sometimes occur during trips to extramural or club sports events, or local, state, regional, or national workshops and conferences. There is an opportunity for open discussions on leadership and individual and group differences any time coaches or staff travel with students for an extended period of time to events or competitions. These conversations do not need to be deep conversations about racial or other differences, as even talking about small differences between students sets the stage for deeper conversations helping students explore their own perspectives as they learn from others. Exposing students to people who do not think the same way as they do can open the door to understanding these differences and creating empathy between student groups.

The NCAA requires all member institutions to offer educational life skills programming to all student-athletes. Offering formal diversity training sessions for all student-athletes will set the foundation for more informal social-cultural conversations. Arguably, the most effective means to facilitating an environment conducive to encouraging informal conversations more organically is to cultivate more diversity within teams by hiring a diverse coaching staff and recruiting a diverse student-athlete population.

Mentoring Relationships

Mentoring relationships are important in the development of leadership capacity. The MSL (Dugan et al., 2013) reports "the degree to which students reported being mentored was directly related to gains in leadership capacity" (p. 12). The report also indicates that the type of mentor affects leadership development based on different racial groups. The report outlines that the following racial groups benefit from the listed type of mentor relationship: (a) faculty mentors: African American/Black, Asian Pacific American, and White students; (b) student affairs mentors: multiracial students; and (c) peer mentors: Latino students (Dugan et al., 2013).

MSL findings (Campbell, Smith, Dugan, & Komives, 2012) demonstrated that "mentorship for personal development was a particularly important predictor of socially responsible leadership capacity. Students who scored higher on the scale indicating that their mentor had helped them to develop personally (e.g., be a positive role model, identify areas for self-improvement) tended to have higher socially responsible leadership capacities" (p. 614). Carow (2013) described positive mentoring relationships as including time commitment and frequency of contact, trust, respect, interpersonal skills, and professional development. Effective mentoring requires a considerable amount of time to develop a relationship. Mutual trust and respect are essential for the mentor and mentee to connect on a deeper level. Interpersonal skills on both sides assist in developing trust and respect. Mentoring relationships may focus on specific recreation or athletic skills or job skills initially, but as the relationship grows the focus may grow into personal development, professional advancement, or leadership development.

Student Employees.   As a supervisor in any collegiate recreation program, there is extensive interaction with student staff. Taking an interest in the development of the student staff creates a mentoring relationship. Professional staff should make efforts to help student staff develop their leadership skills to help them in the performance of their job responsibilities but also to help them develop as individuals. All student staff members move to their own careers and communities (and some will go on to careers in this profession), so we must focus on overall leadership development. Individual meetings with students focusing on their personal development, providing performance evaluations, and giving feedback on job performance can help students develop and may generate the trust and respect necessary for the mentoring relationship to occur.

Club Sports. For club sport officers, mentoring may take the form of helping officers overcome the struggles involved in their respective positions. Club sport officers may be involved in dealing with coaches, players' attitudes, fund-raising, developing budgets, scheduling games, and even being involved in disciplinary action representing their club, in addition to other responsibilities. Acting as a mentor, advisor, or guide, the collegiate recreation professional can work with the student to successfully navigate these contentious areas. By taking an active interest in students and their clubs, the professional can develop that level of trust necessary for the mentoring relationship and guide the student in the development of the skills they need to be successful.

Intercollegiate Athletics. Intercollegiate athletics provides an excellent opportunity to establish meaningful mentoring relationships that originate in an athletic context, but can also develop into relationships that move beyond sport. Coaches have a unique opportunity to become mentors for their players as a result of the nature of the coach–player relationship. Teams also frequently pair first-year players with upper-class students to assist them in the transition to their respective teams. These pairings develop into peer mentoring relationships outside of the athletic context and move into relationships that provide the first-year players with guidance regarding overall transition to college and academic success. Upper-class students serving as peer mentors are also learning and practicing leadership themselves in this mentoring relationship.

Alumni Mentors. Because of the strong alumni base consistent with most athletic programs, local alumni who remain engaged with their respective sports have an even greater propensity to serve as mentors for players who have "been in their shoes," and who may be in careers that they aspire to pursue. These alumni–athlete relationships can encompass mentoring on life as an athlete, academics, professional opportunities, and basic life skills. Working with someone who has already experienced the student-athlete life can assist current athletes in making better choices and developing their leadership skills.

Community Service

The third high-impact recommendation of the MSL report is that "involvement in community service experiences consistently emerge as strong predictors of leadership capacity" (Dugan et al., 2013, p. 15). The report indicates that community service projects have the potential to:

- develop critical group-related skills,
- deepen personal commitments to specific issues,

- build resilience for working in complex systems to create change, and
- disrupt assumptions about social systems and how they operate. (Dugan et al., 2013, p. 15)

The effect of community service on the development of leadership capacity depends on the reflection of the experience. Just completing a community service project is not enough. The participants need to spend time discussing what they did, the importance of what they did, how it affected the organization service is being provided to, how it affects the service participants, and other issues. Sugerman, Doherty, Garvey, and Gass (2000) found that,

> based on educational theories and models, careful reflection is integral to the success of learning. Take away reflection and the individual has a series of experiences that are unconnected and ineffective in changing how he or she learns about the world. (p. 6)

Students can experience a number of different benefits from community service. Celio, Durlak, and Dymnicki (2011) indicated that, "[s]everal research studies suggest that student participation in service learning is associated with positive outcomes in five areas: attitudes toward self, attitudes toward school and learning, civic engagement, social skills, and academic achievement" (p. 165). Improvement in these five areas will also lead to development of leadership skills. Attitudes toward self, school, and learning are important for confidence in leadership skills. Civic engagement will lead to interaction with a variety of different people that can lead to the sociocultural conversations discussed previously.

Community service and philanthropy projects are commonplace on college campuses. Cleaning up roadways, streets, yards, or parks are examples of community service projects. Working with soup kitchens, homeless shelters, or tutoring children are other venues for college students to be engaged in community service projects. Philanthropy projects, on the other hand, are focused upon raising money for some charitable organization like "Relay for Life" or the United Way. Participating in philanthropy projects may also lead to the benefits involved in community service that were noted earlier.

Student Employees.   Contacting the community service office on campus can be a good first step in identifying viable community service options for any program. Organizing student staff to participate in a community service project can lead to greater staff morale and rapport beyond the benefits already identified. Entrusting staff leaders to select an appropriate service site location and organize transportation and details for a successful event will assist in the development of student leadership capacity. Professional staff can employ the mentoring skills discussed previously to guide the student leaders in the implementation of a staff community service project.

Club Sports and Varsity Athletes.   Like fraternities and sororities, club sports teams and varsity athletes can get involved in both community service and philanthropy projects. Making participation in projects of this type mandatory for athletes can increase the likelihood that students will be involved in these projects. Intercollegiate and club athletes can also be involved in different community projects like Learn-to-Skate projects, or other skill development programs associated with their specific sport. Identifying with a specific philanthropy and creating and implementing fundraisers for the philanthropy can create opportunities for these student-athletes to experience the benefits of community service participation. For smaller clubs and teams, creating a general project for all clubs to get involved might be more effective as it may be difficult for smaller clubs to complete a successful project on their own.

Intercollegiate Athletes.   Community service is a valuable and key component to participation in intercollegiate athletics. Many teams set up competitions within respective departments to determine which program accumulates the most community service hours. Although many student-athletes understand that engaging in community service is a "good thing to do," there are few opportunities for meaningful reflection regarding the true significance of what they are doing. To enhance the impact of community service engagement on the growth and development of the student-athlete, coaches/administrators should take time at the beginning of the year to discuss the significance of community service for incoming student-athletes, coaches should provide opportunities for reflection periodically throughout the year, and teams should focus more on the quality or impact of the service completed and less on the total number of hours completed. Student-athletes could also develop their leadership skills if they are included in the identification and planning of team community service initiatives or to target a cause for the year.

Memberships in Off-Campus Organizations

Membership in off-campus organizations allows students the opportunity to apply leadership learning in "real world" environments. The MSL report indicates "off-campus involvement is defined as engaged membership in community-based or work organizations unaffiliated with the college or university" (Dugan et al., 2013, p. 17). This finding may be harder for athletic and recreation programs to implement. Staff will have to intentionally seek opportunities and encourage students to participate. Examples of off-campus organizations include "unions, church groups, parent-teacher associations, and community action groups" (Dugan et al., 2013, p. 17).

In a collegiate recreation setting, the primary off-campus organization with which student leaders are involved is NIRSA: Leaders in Collegiate

Recreation. Attendance at state, regional, and national conferences and serving on work teams can have a profound impact on student leadership development. Involving students in presentations at workshops and conferences can help students gain skills that will help them no matter what their future career might be. Involvement in work teams and governance positions provides an environment for students to network with other students and professionals as well as develop organization and interpersonal skills. Interestingly, attendance at state and regional meetings can include a majority of students and the annual convention and exposition usually includes students as a third of attendees.

Local and state organizations, Boys and Girls Clubs, YMCA and YWCA, after care programs, local sports leagues, and coaching youth sports are additional examples where students might choose to be involved off campus. Student-athletes and collegiate recreation student staff are involved in their respective sports and jobs because they enjoy being active. Sharing this enjoyment of activity with the local community can help provide the students with opportunities to be in leadership positions as well as develop ties and good relationships with the local community.

Membership in off-campus organizations is difficult for student-athletes because of the time requirements for practice and competition. Although student-athletes have less time to engage in memberships in off-campus organizations compared to their nonstudent-athlete counterparts, participation in on-campus or off-campus organizations outside the context of their sport is beneficial for their development of leadership skills. Coaches play a key role in encouraging such involvement by promoting player participation in outside groups and making reasonable allowances for those who wish to become involved.

In addition to the four impact practices, it is imperative for administrators to understand how the practices connect with leadership self-efficacy. The following section discusses the concept briefly, and Chapter 3 elaborates on the developmental readiness of students as they go through the process of developing leadership capacity.

Leadership Self-Efficacy

Leadership self-efficacy (LSE) is one's internal belief in the likelihood that he or she will be successful when engaging in leadership activities. The MSL report indicated "students with low LSE may be unwilling to participate in leadership activities or further develop their skills" (Dugan et al., 2013, p. 20). Those students who do not believe they have the capacity for leadership will not be as inclined to take on leadership roles and will not think of their participation as being part of the leadership process. Collegiate recreation and athletic staff members need to pay special attention to those students who may have low LSE to assist them in gaining confidence in their skills.

Before discussing leadership self-efficacy, it is important to understand self-efficacy. Moen and Federici (2012) indicate "self-efficacy is the aspect of self which refers to how sure (or how confident) the individual is that he or she can successfully perform requisite tasks in specific situations, given one's unique and specific capabilities" (p. 4). Confidence is a key component of self-efficacy. Individuals can have all the skills necessary to be successful, but if they do not believe in themselves they will not be able to put those skills into action.

> LSE (Leadership Self Efficacy) is a person's judgment that he or she can successfully exert leadership by setting a direction for the work group, building relationships with followers in order to gain their commitment to change goals, and working with them to overcome obstacles to change. (Paglis & Green, 2002, p. 217)

Having the capacity to lead is only part of the equation. One must also have confidence in one's skills to lead or engage with others in the leadership process. College students will come with differing levels of skill and confidence in their leadership abilities. It is important that professionals work with students by meeting them where they are developmentally and by providing the right balance of challenge and support. This balance provides a safe environment for developing students' skills and confidence while engaging students in the high-impact practices outlined previously.

Special attention needs to be given to the leadership self-efficacy of female students (Dugan & Komives, 2007). Isaac, Kaatz, Lee, and Carnes (2012) indicate that "several investigators have found that women, particularly at early academic-career stages, are more likely than men to hold low self-efficacy beliefs for leadership" (p. 310). Female students may have the requisite skills to be effective leaders but they may not believe in themselves as much as their male counterparts. Special attention needs to focus on building self-confidence and esteem to assist women in understanding both the positional and relational leader perspectives in taking on positions of leadership.

Collegiate recreation and intercollegiate athletics professionals can help students improve their leadership self-efficacy in the following ways:

- Students need to learn about leadership and what it takes to be a leader.
- Students need to view leadership as a group process and not only the behaviors of a positional leader. Leadership can be both positional and non positional.
- Leadership self-efficacy (LSE) needs to be evaluated. Those students with high LSE can move into positions of leadership and authority and be provided with opportunities to mentor. Those students with low LSE need to be involved in a program to help them increase their LSE and have a more experienced staff person as a mentor.

- Students need opportunities to "practice" leadership in safe environments with limited implications. Employment within collegiate recreation will allow students opportunities to practice learned leadership skills and evaluate how successful they are and what they need to work on to improve.
- Develop a leadership-training program within the department.
- Develop a leadership positional hierarchy where students can progress and move to higher levels of leadership roles within the department.
- Create cross-cultural experiences for students so they can explore themselves and others to gain better understanding of interpersonal relationships.

Student-athletes tend to develop a greater capacity for leadership if they are provided opportunities to take on leadership roles in various capacities within the team. It is important for coaches and administrators to provide student-athletes with resources to assist them in identifying their capacity for being a leader and to provide them with opportunities to learn best practices that can be implemented within their respective teams. Once provided with the foundational knowledge of what it means to be a leader, coaches facilitate student-athlete development in this area by providing athletes with opportunities to be involved in the planning, development, and execution of various aspects of the interworkings of the team. Under the supervision of the coach, players should be permitted to take a greater role in policing themselves and holding themselves and others to established policies and procedures.

NIRSA Leadership Commission

An ever-changing world and higher education landscape have made leadership skills more critical than ever. The changing demographics of campus communities and the nuances of each generation continue to challenge those who lead and those who aspire to lead. Higher education faces an unprecedented period of accelerated change that is driven by shifts in funding models and demands for greater accountability. To respond effectively to the complex educational, social, and economic concerns of society, higher education must develop leaders with the competence to meet the challenges of a constantly changing environment, the ability to think strategically, and a penchant to act collaboratively. (NIRSA, n.d., para 1)

Collegiate recreation has a long history of developing leadership qualities in students and employees. The NIRSA Assembly, part of the NIRSA governance structure, recently identified additional opportunities for NIRSA and NIRSA members to engage in leadership development for the association and for the unique campus communities NIRSA members serve. The NIRSA board formed a commission to analyze leadership development for the association and the field of collegiate recreation. This includes analysis of what it takes to be a leader today, developmental opportunities necessary to become an effective leader, and how to assess the stages of leadership and evaluate the progression of emerging leaders.

As we write this chapter, it is anticipated that the final product of the NIRSA Leadership Commission will be a comprehensive plan for leadership development for both students and professionals. The commission will outline leadership development for the individual and a plan for how departments will implement a leadership development program on their individual campuses.

Conclusion

The NIRSA Leadership Commission continues to work on the ambitious agenda that lies ahead. The commissioners will explore leadership theories and frameworks to now develop appropriate plans and interventions to facilitate appropriate leadership capacity development. These findings should also be shared with athletics administrators as many of the MSL findings can be, and should be, applied in these settings.

References

Baraja-Rohan, A. (1997). Teaching conversations and sociocultural norms with conversation analysis. *Australian Review of Applied Linguistics: Series S, 14,* 71–88.

Campbell, C. M., Smith, M., Dugan, J. P., & Komives, S. R. (2012). Mentors and college student leadership outcomes: The importance of position and process. *Review of Higher Education, 35*(4), 595–625.

Carow, J. (2013). *Positive mentoring relationships: The lived experiences of NIRSA student leadership team members.* Unpublished master's dissertation, University of New Hampshire, Durham.

Celio, C. I., Durlak, J., & Dymnicki, A. (2011). A meta-analysis of the impact of service-learning on students. *Journal of Experiential Education, 34,*164–181.

Dugan, J. P., Kodama, C., Correia, B., & Associates (2013). *Multi-Institutional Study of Leadership insight report: Leadership program delivery.* College Park, MD: National Clearinghouse for Leadership Programs.

Dugan, J. P., & Komives, S. R. (2007). *Developing leadership capacity in college students: Findings from a national study.* College Park, MD: National Clearinghouse for Leadership Programs, University of Maryland.

Dugan, J. P., Torrez, M. A., & Turman, N. T. (2014). *Leadership in intramural sports and club sports: Examining influences to enhance educational impact.* Corvallis, OR: NIRSA.

Edvalson, S. I. (2013). *Sociocultural influences on undergraduate students' conversations on race at a predominantly white institution.* Unpublished doctoral dissertation, University of Iowa, Iowa City.

Isaac, C., Kaatz, A., Lee, B., & Carnes, M. (2012). An educational intervention designed to increase women's leadership self-efficacy. *Life Sciences Education, 11,* 307–322.

Komives, S. R., Dugan, J. P. Owen, J. E., Slack, C., Wagner, W., & Associates. (2011). *The handbook for student leadership development.* San Francisco, CA: Jossey-Bass.

Komives, S. R., Lucas, N., & McMahon, T. (2013). *Exploring leadership for college students who want to make a difference.* San Francisco, CA: Jossey-Bass.
Moen, F., & Federici, R. A. (2012). Perceived leadership self-efficacy and coach competence: Assessing a coaching-based leadership self-efficacy scale. *International Journal of Evidence Based Coaching and Mentoring, 10*(2), 1–16.
NIRSA. (n.d.) *Leadership commission.* Retrieved from http://nirsa.net/nirsa/leadership/volunteer-groups/commissions/leadership-commission/
Paglis, L. L., & Green, S. G. (2002). Leadership self-efficacy and managers' motivation for leading change. *Journal of Organizational Behavior, 23*, 215–235.
Sugerman, D. A., Doherty, K. L., Garvey, D. E., & Gass, M. A. (2000). *Reflective learning: Theory and practice.* Dubuque, IA: Kendall Hunt Publishing Company.
Tyree, T. M. (1998). *Designing an instrument to measure socially responsible leadership using the social change model of leadership development.* Unpublished doctoral dissertation, University of Maryland, College Park.

GORDON M. NESBITT *is an associate professor and director of campus recreation at Millersville University of Pennsylvania.*

ANTHONY GRANT *is an assistant professor and associate director of intercollegiate athletics at Millersville University of Pennsylvania.*

NEW DIRECTIONS FOR STUDENT LEADERSHIP • DOI: 10.1002/yd

3

The Leadership Identity Development (LID) Model (Komives, Owen, Longerbeam, Mainella, & Osteen, 2005) provides a stage leadership development model for college students that can be applied to collegiate recreation student staff, volunteers, participants, and varsity student-athletes. This chapter provides guidance to implement the model in these settings and to create environments that support development.

Linking the Leadership Identity Development Model to Collegiate Recreation and Athletics

Stacey L. Hall

With over 8.1 million students participating in collegiate recreation programs at NIRSA institutions (Forrester, 2014) and over 460,000 students participating in National Collegiate Athletic Association varsity sports (NCAA, 2014), a majority of college students are active on campuses in the United States. For years, collegiate recreation has been touted as a laboratory of learning (Mull, Bayless, & Jamieson, 2005). One of the areas of growth for students is learning and developing leadership.

As described in Chapter 1, the work of professionals in collegiate recreation and athletics is informed by many leadership concepts and models. These models include the Social Change Model of Leadership Development (Higher Education Research Institute, 1996), Relational Leadership (Komives, Lucas, & McMahon, 2013), and Leadership Challenge (Kouzes & Posner, 2006). This chapter focuses on the Leadership Identity Development (LID) model (Komives, Longerbeam, Owen, Mainella, & Osteen, 2006; Komives, Owen, Longerbeam, Mainella, & Osteen, 2005) and relates it to collegiate recreation and athletics programs.

Leader and Leadership Defined

Before exploring the LID model in detail, it is helpful to differentiate the terms leader and leadership (Komives et al., 2013). The terms are not

New Directions for Student Leadership, no. 147, Fall 2015 © 2015 Wiley Periodicals, Inc., A Wiley Company
Published online in Wiley Online Library (wileyonlinelibrary.com) • DOI: 10.1002/yd.20141

interchangeable, although until recently it was common to see the terms used in this way. Leader refers to the individual. "Leader development focuses on individual students' capacity and identity, with or without formal authority, to engage in the leadership process" (Guthrie, Bertrand Jones, Osteen, & Hu, 2013, p. 15). In contrast, leadership refers to the process of the group and the relationships of the group members. The terms are a contrast of position versus process. An underlying assumption of this distinction is that everyone can learn to become a leader. The process is a choice, usually about something in which individuals exhibit care. The difference between leader and leadership will be seen more clearly in the LID model that follows.

Overview of the Leadership Identity Development Model

The LID Model has emerged as a guide for professionals who work with students in the college environment. Komives et al. (2005) developed this model using a grounded theory approach to understand how leadership is developed as a social identity. The study found students followed a process of understanding leadership. The progression in understanding began with seeing leadership as a position exhibited by other people. This view advanced to recognize leadership as a process that involves a whole group. The LID model was developed to understand the complex development that takes place (see Table 3.1). It also serves as a guide for professionals to assist students. The stages of identity progress from awareness to integration/ synthesis. Although this is a linear model in which students progress through the six stages, development is also cyclical where students will continue to have experiences to add depth to their understanding.

The first stage in the LID model is *awareness*. During this stage, students can identify that leadership is around them, typically exhibited by those in positions of authority. Because this stage often occurs during childhood, leaders often include parents, religious leaders, political figures, and historical contributors. Leaders are viewed as other people and students do not see themselves as leaders. Students begin to shift to the next stage when they are challenged to think of what leadership is and to learn more about leaders they see. Often it is triggered by an adult encouraging the student to think more deeply about their role as a leader. Discussions with adults provide an opportunity for students to recognize leadership (Komives et al., 2006).

Typically in elementary and middle school, students shift to the second stage of the LID model, known as *exploration/engagement*. In this stage, students begin to have experiences as a member of a group, such as dance class or band, or youth groups focused on sports, religion, and scouting. During these experiences, adults continue to serve an important role in helping students get more involved in the group, including taking on leadership responsibilities. Another important influence is role modeling by older peers.

Table 3.1   Leadership Identity Development Model

LID Stages	Stage Description	Sample Identity Statement
1. Awareness	Becoming aware of how some people lead and influence others. Usually an external other person, like the U.S. president or a historic figure like Martin Luther King, Jr. *[feels dependent on others]*	A leader is someone out there, not me.
2. Exploration/ Engagement	Immersion in a breadth of group experiences (e.g., Scouts, youth group, swim team) to make friends and find a fit. *[feels dependent on others]*	Maybe I could be a leader.
3. Leader Identified	Fully involved in organizations and groups. Holds a belief that the positional leader does leadership, whereas others do followership. *[may be independent from others (being a leader), dependent on others (being a follower), or hold both views]*	If I am the leader, it is my responsibility to get the job done. If I am a follower, I need to help the leader get the job done.
4. Leadership Differentiated	Recognizes that leadership comes from all around in an organization; as a positional leader, seeks to be a facilitator and practices shared leadership; as a member, knows one is engaged in doing leadership. *[feels interdependent with others]*	I can be *a* leader even if I am not *the* leader and I see that leadership is also a process. We do leadership together.
5. Generativity	Is concerned about the sustainability of the group and seeks to develop others; is concerned about personal passion to leave a legacy and have one's actions make a difference. *[feels interdependent with others]*	We all need to develop leadership in the organization and in others. I am responsible for serving the organization.
6. Integration/ Synthesis	Leadership capacity is an internalized part of oneself and part of the perspective one brings to all situations. *[feels interdependent with others]*	I can work with others to accomplish shared goals and work for change.

Originally published in S. R. Komives, N. Lucas, & T. R. McMahon (2007), *Exploring leadership: For college students who want to make a difference* (2nd ed., pp. 396–397). San Francisco, CA: Jossey-Bass.

Students begin to see those older peers as leaders who do not seem as distant from them. Students begin to transition from this stage when they start to become aware of their potential for leadership. Typically these thoughts begin from role models such as older peers and adults who encourage students by telling them they have potential to be a leader. Students often have an interest in making a difference in the group, so they pursue taking on more responsibility and begin to see the leadership skills they need to develop (Komives et al., 2006).

As students move on to high school and the years following high school, they enter the third stage of the LID model, which is *leader identified*. In this stage, the focus of leadership is on a person in a formal position. Everyone else in the group is a follower. This is a complex stage that can take students longer to master before moving to stage 4. As a result, there are two phases to the stage. First, students focus on role models older than them. A student holding a stage 3 view is typical. Mentors and advisors can help students with that view manage that perspective and allow other students to flourish. Realistically most people including coaches, advisors, and mentors view leadership from a stage 3 view. The mentor can affirm that perspective and show how it can develop to other perspectives. After some time, students begin to experiment serving in a variety of group roles, like delegation and ways to involve members in discussions. As a result, students begin to understand their capacity for leadership (Komives et al., 2006).

In the LID model, the key transition is to shift from stage 3 to stage 4, which is *leadership differentiated*. The significant change is understanding that people in groups are interdependent on each other and that leadership is a group process, where a leader shifts his or her focus to ensuring the entire membership is actively involved in the group's activities. Students also know that leadership can be affiliated with a formal position in a group and also with a member without a formal position. All members of a group can be empowered to influence change in the group (Komives et al., 2006).

During stage 5, known as *generativity*, students' view of leadership continues to expand. Here students broaden their focus from the current activities of the group to the long-term condition of the group. Students think about and plan for the transition to the future leaders of the organization. During this stage, students have developed more of their own leadership identity. Typically as students near the end of their college career, they often take time to reflect on their leadership journey and may also serve as mentors to younger students (Komives et al., 2006).

The final stage in the LID model is *integration/synthesis*. In this stage, students claim a leader identity and are confident they contribute as a leader regardless of their role in the group. Another characteristic of this stage is students develop an appreciation for lifelong learning and development (Komives et al., 2006).

Applying the LID Model

Student affairs professionals should use the LID model to inform their approach to working with students. Specifically, professionals should be equipped to use the LID model in daily work. Additionally, professionals can seek support from colleagues to discuss applications of the model. Upper level students and professionals need to model stages 4, 5, and 6 for students. Role models are influential in the leadership development of others (Komives et al., 2006), therefore professionals and older students need to practice what they are teaching to students. If a professional is in stage 3, he or she is not going to be able to mentor a student who is in stage 5. This places an emphasis on the importance of professionals being equipped to use the model.

With an understanding of the LID model, student affairs professionals are responsible for using the model to inform practice. The professional's role is to help students move through the LID stages. Students arrive on campus at different stages in the model. However, typically college students will be in stage 3 (*leader identified*). For student affairs professionals and athletics administrators, the first step is to assess the current LID stage of a student. This can be accomplished through a series of interventions. From the first interactions with students, professionals can start to gauge what LID stage the student is in. It is helpful to learn about students' experiences prior to becoming a student at the current institution. When students tell their story of leadership involvement and understanding, professionals will begin to assess the proper student stage. Professionals can also ask students to share their definition of leadership in the past and contrast that to their current definition (for example, "What did you use to think leadership was and what do you think it is now?"). It is also revealing to ask students to describe what they believe leadership is through pictures. Each of these strategies can provide insight to the current LID stage of students.

Professionals should equip students with the language of leadership. By seeing the LID model, students enhance their understanding of leadership development as it provides them the terms to express their experience. This transparency helps students learn and progress through the stages.

Reflection plays an important role in the learning process, including building leadership skills. Professionals need to be intentional about creating opportunities for students to reflect on their experiences to help them build their leadership skills. Guthrie and Bertrand Jones (2012) provide a helpful chapter on using reflection in leadership education. Part of the chapter is dedicated to describing specific examples of reflection exercises, including several for a collegiate recreation setting. Reflection activities can include written journals, discussions with staff or fellow students, and case studies that provide an opportunity for role playing (Guthrie & Bertrand Jones, 2012). Written reflection or an intentional dialogue could be scheduled after a shift or during a training session or meeting. The format could be a verbal one-on-one discussion, a 1-minute writing on a notecard, or written log of the season. Professionals can also explore uses of technology, such as blogs for individual reflection (Phelps, 2012). By using the "reflective process, students can better understand themselves and their role in the leadership process" (Guthrie & Bertrand Jones, 2012, p. 59).

New Directions for Student Leadership • DOI: 10.1002/yd

Strategies Specific to Collegiate Recreation and Athletics. As reported in Chapter 2, in a recent report of the findings of the Multi-Institutional Study of Leadership (MSL), four high-impact practices were identified as predictors of building leadership capacity (Dugan, Kodama, Correia, & Associates, 2013). Three of the four can be readily incorporated in collegiate recreation and athletics programs. Sociocultural conversations with peers are an influential experience for students as they build socially responsible leadership capacity. This finding is consistent with an earlier study of student leaders in collegiate recreation, students in formal leadership roles indicated they gained experience working with diverse groups by serving in their leadership role (Hall, Forrester, & Borsz, 2008). Once prepared, professionals should seek opportunities to incorporate sociocultural conversations and reflection of those discussions, including student employee training, club sport officer meetings, and varsity athlete training. To help students advance in the LID model, trained peer leaders can facilitate discussions of sociocultural topics with their peers.

Another high-impact practice is community service activities, which are frequently conducted by club sports, varsity teams, and collegiate recreation student employee groups. To enhance the development opportunities of such experiences, professionals should ensure students are working with the members of the community they are assisting. After the activity, professionals should incorporate reflection exercises into the experience and discuss leadership implications of the students' involvement (Dugan et al., 2013).

The third high-impact practice identified as influential in the study was mentoring relationships. With the amount of contact that professional staff members have with students involved in collegiate recreation and athletics, professionals have an opportunity to discuss the importance of mentoring relationships with students and help students pursue mentorship relationships (Dugan et al., 2013; Hall-Yannessa & Forrester, 2005). To facilitate student advancement in the LID model, professionals should encourage students to develop a succession plan for their club sport, varsity sport, or student employment role.

Another mentoring role that enhances a students' leadership development is the role of experienced students to mentor new students. Professionals need to encourage advanced students to step into the role of a peer mentor. This could include conversations with the student leader to prepare them for being a mentor. Sometimes it is helpful to ask students to recall the impact of peer mentors on their own development. These specific memories can equip the senior student to serve in this important role as peer mentor. A frequently used strategy is to incorporate peers into the delivery of training material for volunteer or paid positions in the organization. Last, professionals can develop and implement training sessions on how to mentor peers (Dugan et al., 2013).

Strategies for Students in Roles of Responsibility.   When students serve in roles with significant level of commitment and responsibility, professionals have more ability during the course of the role to provide opportunities for more impact on students' development. These roles include club sport members, varsity athletes, student employees, and volunteers serving as club sport officers, advisory board members, and interns. Position descriptions for these roles should contain learning outcomes of each role and incorporate the language of the LID model. Incorporating potential outcomes will increase the chance students will learn them. When facilitating transition processes, professionals should use peer mentor groups to aid in the process. This provides visible leadership for older peers to help trigger the shift from stage 3 to stage 4 of the LID model. For formal positions in which students serve for a specific amount of time, there are opportunities for formal discussions with professional staff. Incorporating elements of reflection and the LID model into performance review process can provide significant impact, particularly for student volunteers, student employees, and varsity athletes.

When working with established groups and organizations, such as a varsity team, club sport, or an advisory board, note that most college students will begin in stage 3. As a result, the professional can ensure specific skills are actively incorporated into the group, including delegating tasks, facilitating effective meetings, and developing goals for the group (Komives et al., 2006).

Challenges Implementing the LID

Although the LID model provides guidance for professionals who work with students, there are some important challenges to note. First, when assessing the LID stage students are in, it is possible for the student to describe his or her understanding of leadership of an advanced stage (Owen, 2012). Yet the behavior may not match the articulated stage. That student may talk about teamwork and collaboration but exhibits an authoritarian style of telling people what to do. This situation calls for a professional to be observant and to follow up with the student on specific incidents that are incongruent. Until assessment tools are developed to thoroughly determine students' current stage, accurately identifying the stage is challenging.

Second, professionals should use caution when applying a model to all students. Not only do students arrive on campus at different stages, as mentioned earlier, but there can be differences based on the race or ethnicity of a student. Research shows differences in "predictors of leadership development across racial groups." (Dugan, Kodama, & Gebhart, 2012, p. 184). Although more research is needed to further understand the differences, professionals should encourage sociocultural conversations among students, as those conversations have a positive impact on all students.

Last, professionals should understand college student development theory related to psychosocial and cognitive perspectives. This could determine the appropriate time for integrating leadership development with existing student development theories to identify opportunities for students based on developmental readiness. Each student has a different degree to which they are prepared and motivated to expand their leadership knowledge, skills, attributes, and abilities (Dugan et al., 2013). Understanding the unique situation of each student emphasizes the need for a variety of strategies to facilitate progression within the LID model, rather than a "one size fits all" approach.

Conclusion

The recent scholarship in the area of leadership development provides a sound platform for professionals to employ the LID model to collegiate recreation and athletics on campus. The LID model provides a helpful tool for practitioners to use in these settings. This work also reinforces the impact of professionals working with students in these settings can have on students' leadership development.

References

Dugan, J. P., Kodama, C. M., Correia, B., & Associates. (2013). *Multi-institutional study of leadership insight report: Leadership program delivery*. College Park, MD: National Clearinghouse for Leadership Programs.

Dugan, J. P., Kodama, C. M., & Gebhart, M. C. (2012). Race and leadership development among college students: The additive value of collective racial esteem. *Journal of Diversity in Higher Education, 5*, 174–189.

Forrester, S. A. (2014). *Benefits of campus recreational sports participation*. Corvallis, OR: NIRSA.

Guthrie, K. L., & Bertrand Jones, T. (2012, Winter). Teaching and learning: Using experiential learning and reflection for leadership education. In K. L. Guthrie & L. Osteen (Eds.), *New Directions for Student Services: No. 140. Developing students' leadership capacity* (pp. 53–63). San Francisco, CA: Jossey-Bass.

Guthrie, K. L., Bertrand Jones, T., Osteen, L., & Hu, S. (2013). *Cultivating leader identity and capacity in students from diverse backgrounds* (Vol. 39). Hoboken, NJ: Wiley.

Hall, S. L., Forrester, S. A., & Borsz, M. (2008). A constructivist case study examining the leadership development of undergraduate students in campus recreational sports. *Journal of College Student Development, 49*, 125–140.

Hall-Yannessa, S. L., & Forrester, S. A. (2005). Impact of advisor interaction on the development of leadership skills in club sports officers. *Recreational Sports Journal, 29*(1), 9–21.

Higher Education Research Institute [HERI]. (1996). *A social change model of leadership development: Guidebook* (Ver. III). College Park, MD: National Clearinghouse for Leadership Programs.

Komives, S. R., Longerbeam, S. D., Owen, J. E., Mainella, F. C., & Osteen, L. (2006). A leadership identity development model: Applications from a grounded theory. *Journal of College Student Development, 47*, 401–420.

Komives, S. R., Lucas, N., & McMahon, T. R. (2007). *Exploring leadership: For college students who want to make a difference* (2nd ed.). San Francisco, CA: Jossey-Bass.

Komives, S. R., Lucas, N., & McMahon, T. R. (2013). *Exploring leadership: For college students who want to make a difference* (3rd ed.). San Francisco, CA: John Wiley & Sons, Inc.

Komives, S. R., Owen, J. E., Longerbeam, S. D., Mainella, F. C., & Osteen, L. (2005). Developing a leadership identity: A grounded theory. *Journal of College Student Development, 46*, 593–611.

Kouzes, J. M., & Posner, B. Z. (2006). *Leadership challenge: How to make extraordinary things happen in organizations* (4th ed.). San Francisco, CA: Jossey-Bass.

Mull, R. F., Bayless, K. G., & Jamieson, L. M. (2005). *Recreational sport management* (4th ed.). Champaign, IL: Human Kinetics.

National Collegiate Athletic Association [NCAA]. (2014, November 4). *Current student-athletes.* Retrieved from http://www.ncaa.org/student-athletes/current

Owen, J. E. (2012, Winter). Using student development theories as conceptual frameworks in leadership education. *New Directions for Student Services, 140*, 17–35.

Phelps, K. (2012, Winter). Leadership online: Expanding the horizon. In K. L. Guthrie & L. Osteen (Eds.), *New Directions for Student Services: No. 140. Developing students' leadership capacity* (pp. 65–75). San Francisco, CA: Jossey-Bass.

STACEY L. HALL *is the director of campus recreation at the University of New Hampshire.*

NEW DIRECTIONS FOR STUDENT LEADERSHIP • DOI: 10.1002/yd

4

This chapter discusses the transition from high school to college for student-athletes. The concepts of athlete identity and leadership development are discussed through the lens of the high school athlete who attends college as a collegiate athlete and those students who are dealing with a loss of their high school athlete identity.

Opportunities and Challenges for First-Year Student-Athletes Transitioning From High School to College

Joy Gaston Gayles, Ashley R. Baker

The transition from high school to college for student-athletes is complex and filled with anxiety and excitement about what it means to be a college student and a college athlete. One of the major challenges for high school student-athletes involves the art of balancing academic, athletic, and social roles and responsibilities in the midst of resolving the transition experiences faced by all incoming students that include social adjustment, loneliness, and stress. In this chapter we focus on what student-athletes should expect moving from high school to college. We begin with a brief discussion on the high school athletic experience and what is involved in the process of participating at the college level and conclude with a discussion of what student-athletes can expect as incoming college first-year students. We identify some of the major development tasks students will face during the transition process and how college administrators can facilitate growth and learning in ways that create opportunities out of developmental challenges.

High School Student-Athlete Experience

During the 2012–2013 school year, more than 7.7 million teens in the United States competed in high school sports (National Federation of State High School Associations, 2014). Interscholastic sports are considered one of the most important activities sponsored by high schools. As a result, research shows adolescents place a high value on sports participation and sports provides a valued place for them within their high school community

New Directions for Student Leadership, no. 147, Fall 2015 © 2015 Wiley Periodicals, Inc., A Wiley Company
Published online in Wiley Online Library (wileyonlinelibrary.com) • DOI: 10.1002/yd.20142

(Larson, 2000). Participation on a school sports team can bring increased recognition and reward to students. This recognition often builds their self-confidence and enhances their popularity in school and within the local community (Coakley, 2009; Eccles & Barber, 1999).

There are many benefits to participation in sports for high school students. In general high school students who participate in sports tend to perform better academically than their nonathlete peers, have reduced dropout rates, are more interested in attending college, and report more positive educational experiences (Hartmann, 2008; Marsh & Kleitman, 2003). Coakley (2009) contends that parents, coaches, and teachers add an additional layer of encouragement and confidence building to the lives of athletes that may not exist for other students. High school athletes' academic experiences are closely monitored through homework checks, grade checks, and mandatory study hall sessions.

Sport participation also provides high school athletes with the opportunity to develop and display leadership qualities (Dobosz & Beaty, 1999). Snyder and Spreitzer's (1992) study revealed evidence that athletic participation appears to increase the capacity to lead others. Further, the study suggests that athletes possess stronger leadership skills compared to nonathletes. Communicating with their teammates and coaches, role modeling good behavior and work ethic, building rapport with their peers, and serving as a team captain are various leadership roles and behaviors high school and college athletes may take on in sports. As high school athletes transition to college, these leadership roles may shift, especially when encountering the challenges of being a first-year student and athlete.

Although there are many benefits to sports participation, there are some challenges, particularly for elite athletes who are especially talented in their sport (Coakley, 2009). Many of the athletes with elite talent participate in sports year round, and they become overly dedicated to sports at the expense of other activities. Consequently, many high school athletes spend much of their high school career focused on receiving an athletic scholarship. The reality is that an estimated average of 5% of high school seniors will have an opportunity to fill an open first-year roster spot on a college team (National Conference Athletics Association [NCAA], 2013).

Highly talented high school athletes who are fortunate to continue athletic participation in college will be faced with a host of factors they must consider in the college selection process. In consultation with parents and coaches, high school athletes can confidently navigate a potentially overwhelming recruiting process. Recruiting plays an important role in this decision-making process and has become more complex over the years as it requires year-round involvement by the coaches, athletes, and parents. With so few roster spots available for high school athletes looking to compete in college athletics, the recruitment process is a way for coaches and athletes to find the best fit for their respective needs.

Recruitment Process

For high school athletes aspiring to participate in college athletics, the recruiting process shapes the college decision-making process. College coaches are looking for the best athletes to recruit for their teams. The recruiting process is a tool used for identifying and evaluating high school athletes with the intent to persuade high school athletes to commit to attending the coach's institution and participating on their athletic team. The NCAA recruitment process and the regulations that coaches and athletes must follow vary depending on the sport and division. The NCAA recruiting guidelines differ for Division I football, Division I men's basketball, Division I women's basketball, Division I other sports, Division II, and Division III and are not enforced until an athlete begins taking ninth-grade classes (NCAA, 2014a). For example, according to NCAA Bylaw 13.02.8, Division I men's basketball coaches are allowed 130 recruiting-person days per academic year, whereas Bylaw 13.02.9 states Division I women's basketball coaches are permitted only 112 days (NCAA, 2014a). Throughout the recruiting process, athletes are encouraged to make preparations for enrollment at the collegiate level. One step necessary in this transition to college as an athlete requires registration with the NCAA Eligibility Center (NCAA, 2014b), whose staff is responsible for certifying all incoming athletes prior to the start of their first year of college.

The First-Year College Athlete

Transitioning from high school to college can be a challenging and complex experience for first-year students, particularly for special populations of first-year students such as first generation, at-risk, low-income, and student-athletes (Terenzini et al., 1994). Theories of college impact identify a range of factors that influence the transition process and the overall college experience, such as background characteristics and aptitude, students' initial goals and commitments, academic and social experiences in college, interactions with faculty, staff, and peers, and relationships with individuals, and groups outside of college, for example, parents, employers, and community organizations (Clark, 2005; Tinto, 1993, 1999). Transition theories, such as Schlossberg's theory (Evans, Forney, Guido, Patton, & Renn, 2009), are also helpful in understanding the student-athlete transition from high school to college. Moving from high school to college is one of many life transitions for this population. Schlossberg's theory is particularly useful for managing anticipated, unanticipated, and nonevent (e.g., anticipated transitions that do not occur) transitions and what changes one might expect relative to relationships, routines, assumptions, and roles. Schlossberg refers to moving in, moving through, and moving out as pivotal points along the transition process and recommends the 4 S strategy for coping with the difficulty of transitions through examining dimensions of the self, situation, strategies, and supports (Evans et al., 2009).

The transition from high school to college includes adapting to the academic and social norms of the institution (Tinto, 1993, 1999). This process can be difficult, especially for student-athletes who have constraints on their time and energy due to the demands of athletic participation. The literature consistently suggests that involvement, defined as the amount of physical and psychological energy invested into the academic and social systems within the institution, is connected to successfully navigating the challenges associated with the first-year experience. Further, student involvement has been linked to positive outcomes such as academic and social integration as well as persistence (Astin, 1993).

Challenges and Opportunities for Incoming College Athletes

Once student-athletes are recruited and cleared by the NCAA to participate in college sports, there are a variety of adjustment and adaption experiences that characterize the transition process. Adjusting and adapting to college refer to students' ability to meet the academic and social demands of attending college (Melendez, 2006, 2009). Much like all first-year students, student-athletes can expect to experience challenges and opportunities moving from high school to college. It is important to note that student-athletes are distinct from incoming students in the general student population because they must learn to balance athletic, academic, and social demands of the college experience. Nonetheless, student-athletes are expected to make gains in student learning and personal development during the college years in ways similar to their nonathlete peers.

Participation in college sports has the potential to facilitate the development of skills that are transferrable to other domains such as identity, multicultural, moral, and cognitive, and leadership development (Simons, Van Rheenen, & Covington, 1999). Learning how to win and lose, for example, requires skill development and character building that is linked to psychosocial developmental areas such as managing emotions like pride and shame, sadness and excitement, and anger and happiness. In many ways, the same skills employed for learning plays and techniques to execute on game days require a similar amount time, effort, and energy necessary for studying and mastering material in preparation for an exam. Further, participating in college sports has the potential to foster leadership development (Wright & Côté, 2003). We discuss some of the challenges and opportunities for first-year student-athletes in the following section.

Challenges

During the first-year of college, student-athletes will be challenged by demands on their time and energy in three important domains—academic, athletic, and social. In the academic domain, student-athletes, particularly at the Division I level, are expected to take a full load of classes and make sufficient progress toward degree completion each year. Failure to make satisfactory academic progress and maintain a minimum grade point average will result in loss of eligibility for sport participation. Student-athletes are also expected to practice 20 hours per week and compete during competition season, which often involves hours of travel time for away games. The demands of the academic and athletic domains leave very little time for social involvement; yet, research supports that social involvement, particularly with nonathlete peers, is associated with gains in cognitive and affective development (Astin, 1993; Gayles & Hu, 2009). Although student-athletes will experience challenges in these three domains, it is critical for student-athletes to strike a balance among these three domains and avoid role engulfment. Role engulfment refers to overidentification with athletic roles and responsibilities at the expense of adequate identification with academic roles and responsibilities (Adler, 1991). The good news is that many of the challenges experienced during the first year can be turned into opportunities for leadership and personal development for student-athletes.

Opportunities

When balanced well, participation in intercollegiate athletics has the potential to ease the transition from high school to college, as well as facilitate growth and development (Astin, 1993; Melendez, 2006; Miller & Kerr, 2003). It is common for first-year students to be anxious about the social adjustment to college life. However, participation in college sports facilitates bonding with peers (for example teammates) that can reduce feelings of isolation and stress as well as ease the social adjustment to college life (Melendez, 2006). Further, participation in college sports is a great opportunity for students to form relationships and practice effective communication with people unlike themselves as a result of the high level of diversity within and across teams (Howard-Hamilton & Sina, 2001; Pascarella, Bohr, Nora, & Terenzini, 1995; Toma, Wolf-Wendel, & Morphew, 2001). Through participating on athletic teams that are diverse, student-athletes report high levels of openness to diversity and difference in ways unparalleled to the larger campus community (Pascarella et al., 1995; Toma et al., 2001).

In summary, three conditions are necessary to facilitate student learning and personal development during the college years (Evans et al., 2009; Sanford, 1966). First, students must be ready to grow, suggesting that individuals will not change in positive ways until they are ready to do so. Second, individuals must be properly challenged within the environment in ways that interrupt one's equilibrium and stimulates movement to a higher or more complex way of thinking and dealing with complicated situations. Many of the issues and problems faced by student-athletes can be considered developmental tasks that are necessary to foster growth and development in cognitive and affective areas of adolescent development. Too much challenge, however, can have adverse effects on student learning and personal growth. Finally, in order to maximize learning and development, students must be supported with the environment. Much like challenge, too much support from the environment can be detrimental to growth and learning. College coaches and athletic and university administrators must intentionally work with student-athletes where they are individually in ways that provide optimal levels of challenge and support to facilitate positive growth and development.

Student Development During the College Years

Student-athletes are expected to experience growth and development in key areas during the college years. Moreover, there is great concern over the extent to which student-athletes benefit from the college experiences in ways similar to their nonathlete peers (Bowen & Levin, 2003; Shulman & Bowen, 2011). Thus, athletic administrators and other campus administrators who work closely with student-athletes should be aware of the developmental tasks student-athletes will face as they transition to college. Such knowledge and awareness can be used to help facilitate growth and development for student-athletes in the context of the challenges and opportunities they will face. In addition to knowledge and awareness about how students grow and change during college, athletic administrators must be equipped to challenge and support student-athletes in ways that facilitate growth and development (Sanford, 1966). Participation in intercollegiate athletics will present many opportunities to challenge and support student-athletes. However, it is important to note that too much challenge without enough support and too much support without enough challenge can actually be harmful for growth and development. Thus, administrators must strike the proper balance that allows student-athletes to grapple with developmental crises and new information in ways that stimulate positive growth. Student development theories are useful in that they convey important ways in which students are expected to grow and change and direction for how to facilitate positive growth and development during the college years.

Two important areas in which students are expected to grow and develop are psychosocial and cognitive. Psychosocial development involves the content of development (Evans et al., 2009). The developmental tasks associated with psychosocial growth involve developing skills and the capacity to define oneself in a positive healthy way, communicate and work effectively with others, and make commitments and express values that reflect one's identity. Chickering and Reisser (1993) developed seven vectors that detail developmental tasks that students grapple with during the adolescent years—developing competence, managing emotions, moving through autonomy toward interdependence, establishing identity, developing purpose, and developing integrity all of which relate to developing their leadership capacity. Other psychosocial theories articulate the importance of experiencing a period of crisis before making commitments across multiple domains as well as the consequences of making commitments without exploring and not engaging in the process at all (Josselson, 1987; Marcia, 1966).

Cognitive development represents another area in which students are expected to grow and change in positive ways during the college years. This family of student development theories focuses on *how* individuals make meaning of their experiences, that is, how people perceive, organize, and evaluate experiences and events that happen in their lives (Evans et al., 2009). As individuals are presented with new, often conflicting, information that challenges their current way of thinking, they must move to a high level of reasoning in order to make sense of the new ideas and new information. Perry's (1999) scheme of intellectual development outlines nine schemas that describe how individuals make meaning that move from black and white, right and wrong thinking, to becoming comfortable with multiple realities and ultimately using evidence to weigh multiple arguments as better than or worse than.

Moral development is also a part of the cognitive structural family of theories but focuses specifically on how individuals reason about moral dilemmas. Kohlberg's theory (Kohlberg & Hersh, 1977) of moral development describes three phases of moral development that move from preconventional reasoning to postconventional reasoning. An easier way to think about the phases of the theory is to consider the justification attached to reasoning about moral dilemmas (as opposed to focusing on the moral decision). For instance, individuals using preconventional reasoning focus on the personal consequences (avoiding punishment, maintaining self-image) as the basis for moral thinking, whereas someone using postconventional reasoning has the capacity to use universal principles that supersede self and focus on the greater good as the basis for moral thinking. When student-athletes face developmental tasks that require them to make intellectual decisions or consider the consequences of their actions, knowledge about cognitive-structural theories can be useful for helping students grow in positive ways from their personal experiences.

Conclusion

The transition process from high school to college is filled with a great deal of uncertainty and can be a scary and exciting time in the lives of most students. Student-athletes represent a special population of college students that experience adjustment and adaption challenges like their nonathlete peers as well as challenges balancing participation in college sport with academic responsibilities and social life. The better university administrators understand the unique challenges faced by student-athletes the better they will be able to serve this population and help them make the most of their college experience and experience gains in student learning and personal development.

References

Adler, P. A. (1991). *Backboards & blackboards: College athletics and role engulfment*. New York, NY: Columbia University Press.

Astin, A. W. (1993). *What matters in college?: Four critical years revisited*. San Francisco, CA: Jossey-Bass.

Bowen, W. G., & Levin, S. A. (2003). *Reclaiming the game: College sports and educational values*. Princeton, NJ: Princeton University Press.

Chickering, A. W., & Reisser, L. (1993). *Education and identity* (2nd ed.). San Francisco, CA: Jossey-Bass.

Clark, M. R. (2005). Negotiating the freshman year: Challenges and strategies among first-year college students. *Journal of College Student Development, 46*, 296–316.

Coakley, J. (2009). *Sports in society: Issues and controversies* (10th ed.). New York, NY: McGraw-Hill.

Dobosz, R., & Beaty, L. (1999). The relationship between athletic participation and high school students' leadership ability. *Adolescence, 34*, 215–220.

Eccles, J. S., & Barber, B. L. (1999). Student council, volunteering, basketball, or marching band—what kind of extracurricular involvement matters? *Journal of Adolescent Research, 14*(10), 10–43.

Evans, N. J., Forney, D. S., Guido, F. M., Patton, D. L., & Renn, K. A. (2009). *Student development in college: Theory, research, and practice*. San Francisco, CA: Jossey-Bass.

Gayles, J. G., & Hu, S. (2009). The influence of student engagement and sport participation on college outcomes among Division I student-athletes. *Journal of Higher Education, 80*, 315–333.

Hartmann, D. (2008). *High school sports participation and educational attainment: Recognizing, assessing, and utilizing the relationship*. Report to the LA84 Foundation. Retrieved from http://thesocietypages.org/files/2013/03/HighSchoolSportsParticipation1.pdf

Howard-Hamilton, M. F., & Sina, J. A. (2001). How college affects student-athletes. In M. F. Howard-Hamilton & S. K. Watt (Eds.), *New Directions for Student Services: No. 93. Student Services for Athletes* (pp. 35–45). San Francisco, CA: Jossey-Bass.

Josselson, R. (1987). *Finding herself: Pathways to identity development in women*. San Francisco, CA: Jossey-Bass.

Kohlberg, L., & Hersh, R. H. (1977). Moral development: A review of the theory. *Theory Into Practice, 16*(2), 53–59.

Larson, R. W. (2000). Toward a psychology of positive youth development. *American Psychologist, 55*(1), 170–178.

Marcia, J. E. (1966). Development and validation of ego-identity status. *Journal of Personality and Social Psychology, 3*, 551–558.

Marsh, H., & Kleitman, S. (2003). School athletic participation: Mostly gain with little pain. *Journal of Sport and Exercise Psychology, 25*, 205–228.

Melendez, M. C. (2006). The influence of athletic participation on the college adjustment of freshmen and sophomore student-athletes. *Journal of College Student Retention: Research, Theory and Practice, 8*, 39–55.

Melendez, M. C. (2009). Psychosocial influences on college adjustment in Division I student-athletes: The role of athletic identity. *Journal of College Student Retention: Research, Theory and Practice, 11*, 345–361.

Miller, P. S., & Kerr, G. A. (2003). The role experimentation of intercollegiate student athletes. *Sport Psychologist, 17*(2), 196–219.

National Federation of State High School Associations. (2014). *2012–13 high school athletics participation survey results.* Retrieved from http://www.nfhs.org/Participation Statics/PDF/2013-14%20NFHS%20Handbook_pgs52-70.pdf

NCAA. (2013). *Probability of competing beyond high school.* Indianapolis, IN: The National Collegiate Athletic Association. Retrieved from http://www.ncaa.org/about /resources/research/probability-competing-beyond-high-school

NCAA. (2014a). *2013–2014 Division I manual.* Indianapolis, IN: The National Collegiate Athletic Association. Retrieved from http://www.ncaapublications.com /productdownloads/D114.pdf

NCAA (2014b). *2013–2014 guide for the college-bound student-athlete.* Indianapolis, IN: The National Collegiate Athletic Association. Retrieved from http://www .ncaapublications.com/productdownloads/CBSA.pdf

Pascarella, E. T., Bohr, L., Nora, A., & Terenzini, P. T. (1995). Intercollegiate athletic participation and freshman-year cognitive outcomes. *Journal of Higher Education, 66,* 369–387.

Perry, W. G. (1999). *Forms of intellectual and ethical development in the college years: A scheme.* San Francisco, CA: Jossey-Bass.

Sanford, N. (1966). *Self and society: Social change and individual development.* New York, NY: Atherton Press.

Shulman, J. L., & Bowen, W. G. (2011). *The game of life: College sports and educational values.* Princeton, NJ: Princeton University Press.

Simons, H. D., Van Rheenen, D., & Covington, M. V. (1999). Academic motivation and the student-athlete. *Journal of College Student Development, 40,* 151–162.

Snyder, E., & Spreitzer, E. (1992). Scholars and athletes. *Youth and Society, 23,* 510–522.

Terenzini, P. T., Rendon, L. I., Upcraft, M. L., Millar, S. B., Allison, K. W., Gregg, P. L., et al. (1994). The transition to college: Diverse students, diverse stories. *Research in Higher Education, 35,* 57–73.

Tinto, V. (1993). *Leaving college: Rethinking the causes and cures of student attrition* (2nd ed.). Chicago, IL: University of Chicago.

Tinto, V. (1999). Taking retention seriously: Rethinking the first year of college. *NACADA Journal, 19*(2), 5–9.

Toma, J. D., Wolf-Wendel, L., & Morphew, C. C. (2001). There's no "I" in "team": Lessons from athletics on community building. *Review of Higher Education, 24,* 369–396.

Wright, A., & Côté, J. (2003). A retrospective analysis of leadership development through sport. *Sport Psychologist, 17,* 268–291.

Joy Gaston Gayles *is an associate professor in the College of Education at North Carolina State University.*

Ashley R. Baker *is a doctoral student in the sport management and policy program in the Department of Kinesiology at the University of Georgia.*

New Directions for Student Leadership • DOI: 10.1002/yd

5

The chapter explores student-athlete campus engagement and challenges faced by athletes that may impede leadership development. The roles of athletic academic advisors, team coaches, and teammates in leadership development are outlined. Current campus initiatives directly related to intercollegiate athlete leadership development are also shared.

Intercollegiate Athlete as Student Leader

Anthony Weaver, Kathleen Simet

College athletics is a results-oriented effort typically measured by tangible outcomes—wins and losses. Unlike many other students, intercollegiate student-athletes' effort and results are seen and judged by millions on a day-by-day, game-by-game basis, creating a pressure that few can truly understand. Teams can fall short for many reasons such as poor recruiting, unsuccessful player development, injuries, or bad coaching decisions. The difference between success and failure is miniscule, sometimes based on the execution, or lack thereof, of one player or one play during one game. However, as coaches reflect on the results of a season, rarely do they feel as though it was all based on one situation. Coaches often cite big picture issues, such as the lack of leadership, as one of the key downfalls to an unsuccessful season. Knowing that leadership is one of the most important determinants of a team's success, college athletic departments should consider leadership development programs for their student-athletes.

This chapter provides a snapshot of leadership development in college athletics, the role of a student-athlete leader, and the importance of self-leadership. It also discusses the strategies of a successful leadership development program, with a special focus on two high-impact practices for leadership development capacity: sociocultural conversations and the role of mentors in the athletic department. Best practices in leadership development programs conclude the section.

Leadership Development in College Athletics

Although the number of leadership programs has increased across college campuses, one area that is still relatively new to implementing an

NEW DIRECTIONS FOR STUDENT LEADERSHIP, no. 147, Fall 2015 © 2015 Wiley Periodicals, Inc., A Wiley Company
Published online in Wiley Online Library (wileyonlinelibrary.com) • DOI: 10.1002/yd.20143

organized leadership development program has been intercollegiate athletics. Athletics offers perhaps one of the best practical venues to implement and practice leadership development. Because student-athletes usually commit to an organized group (their team) for their entire college experience, the intercollegiate athletics' team structure presents an existing framework that lends itself nicely with the application of thorough leadership development programs, in particular those programs grounded in sound theory.

Widely held research related to leadership in athletics focuses primarily on the development of coaches' leadership styles (Sullivan & Kent, 2010) versus developing student-athlete leadership capacity. The structure in athletics usually allows for slow steady growth as an athlete, which also can allow for purposeful growth as a positional leader. However, the traditional approach to leadership in sport for students has been for teams to identify student-athlete leaders and give them the title of captain. There are two ways a student-athlete usually becomes a captain.

First, athletes can serve their time, gain more experience, and work their way into a position of authority. Being a collegiate athlete has almost an inherent hierarchy, where new student-athletes put in their 4 years and by the time a student-athlete is a senior, he or she is often expected to serve in a positional leadership role or specifically as team captain, simply because of experience. However, time alone does not teach young people how to be leaders, yet student-athletes are often placed in these leadership roles without any knowledge, skills, or competencies for navigating the unfamiliar leadership terrain. Duke University Men's Head Basketball Coach, Mike Krzyzewski, cautions:

> What I try to do is not assume that just because the oldest person is the oldest that he is the leader. You hope that they are because they have the most experience, but not everybody on a team is a leader or wants to be a leader. (Sitkin & Hackman, 2011, p. 495)

Another common approach for a student-athlete to earn a leadership role is by being a top athlete (Yukelson, Weinberg, Jackson, & Richardson, 1983). It is often assumed that the top performers, who have garnered the athletic respect of their teammates, will be able to lead the team through tough competition simply by rallying their team to success. However, being a star athlete does not necessitate that he or she will be a star leader. Being a leader on and off the field requires more than just athletic performance. It requires the individual not only to complete tasks, be respectful, and have confidence but also to influence other team members to do the same. Lowney (2003) said it best, "raw talent and sheer ambition didn't always translate into long-term success" (p. 2). The same is true for leadership.

The Role of the Student-Athlete as Leader

Any coach will state that, next to athletic talent, one of the top character-istics they seek and value in a student-athlete is leadership. Simply put, a coach needs a leader to help win. For most athletic teams, the coach is often on the opposite end of the court or field and unable to speak to his or her team in some of the most crucial game moments. Having a leader on the field, court, or rink in the crucial moment of a game often means the team will rise to the challenge and score a game winning point, make strategic defensive decisions, maintain composure under pressure, keep a positive attitude, and temporarily fill the shoes of the coach.

Strong leadership can provide the obvious athletic benefit of winning, but there are also the benefits outside of sport that a leader can have on his or her team. Team captains take on "behind the scene" responsibili-ties such as being a role model and mentoring teammates, structuring cap-tain's practice and off-season workouts, making sure teammates fulfill their own responsibilities, and follow team rules (Dupuis, Bloom, & Loughead, 2006). In some cases, captains are expected to be problem solvers including dealing with discipline issues. In addition, the captain is provided unique access to coaches, which allows a student-athlete the opportunity to work with the team's decision-makers. Often captains will act as a mediator be-tween the coaching staff and the student-athletes when it comes to dis-cussing team related issues (Day, Sin, & Chen, 2004). Because captains are given a tremendous amount of responsibilities from both their teammates and their coaches, they should be given the proper leadership training to be successful.

Implementation: A Focus on High-Impact Practices

It should not be assumed that most student-athletes will just be "ready" to handle a leadership role when it is their time. Athletic departments should foster leadership development and continuously work with promis-ing student-athletes. Creating and promoting opportunities that can help advance a student-athlete's leadership development are essential for suc-cess. For instance, athletic teams can implement a leadership development program that uses the high-impact practices for building leadership capac-ity identified in the Multi-Institutional Study of Leadership (MSL) as dis-cussed previously in Chapters 2 and 3 (Dugan, Kodama, Correia, & As-sociates, 2013). Here we discuss two of the high-impact practices that are strongly associated with gains in leadership development and can easily be highlighted in most college athletic leadership programs: sociocultural con-versations and developing mentoring relationships.

High-Impact Practices: Sociocultural Conversations. Sport acts as a common denominator that brings people from different back-grounds together under the common umbrella of sport participation

(Cunningham, 2007). Although diversity in college athletics and across higher education is still a work in progress, most coaches recruit student-athletes with the commitment to one common goal—winning. As recruiting budgets at schools and the need to identify talented players have increased, coaches have had the luxury of finding talent from around the world. In some cases, athletic grants-in-aid allow schools to cover the full cost of tuition, room and board, and other expenses for student-athletes who are athletically gifted yet would not be able to afford the cost of college otherwise. These factors have allowed coaches from all divisions of NCAA sports to expand their recruiting base to a diverse population.

It is not uncommon for teams to have student-athletes who differ in many ways: racially, religiously, and economically to name a few. This small group of diverse individuals that come together allows student-athletes the perfect laboratory to learn about others who are very different from them. Once assembled, student-athletes, regardless of socioeconomic background, become a member of another group—the team. Research indicates that for many, this group becomes a powerful identity for the student-athlete. Student-athletes define themselves "first and foremost as athletes" and not as a member of a racial group (Brown, Jackson, Brown, Sellers, Keiper, & Manuel, 2003, p. 165).

Although winning may be the main reason for improving the diversity on a team, coaches have created an environment for leadership development. Creating a diverse team lends itself nicely to one of the high-impact practices for building leadership capacity, sociocultural conversations. In fact, the Dugan et al. (2013) MSL study found that "socio-cultural conversations with peers are the *single strongest predictor* of socially responsible leadership capacity for students across demographic groups" (p. 9). Athletic departments and, in particular, coaches should embrace conversations and programs that highlight diversity, allowing student-athletes to examine different points of view and develop new ways of thinking about their own leadership style. Using a complimentary model such as the Relational Leadership Model (discussed in Chapter 1) provides administrators and coaches a framework to infuse opportunities to focus on relationship building rather than just the end goal of winning a game. For instance, at the University of Wisconsin-Madison, the athletic department has created the Diversity and Inclusion Program, which offers several programs throughout the year for student-athletes to gain a deeper appreciation of building diverse relationships. Opportunities such as the Academic Athletic Mentor Partnership (AAMP), the Diversity Forum, and the Student-Athletes Equally Supporting Others (SAESO) are just some examples of how the University of Wisconsin-Madison has created an environment that produces beneficial sociocultural conversations used to develop socially responsible leaders (University of Wisconsin, 2014).

High-Impact Practices: Mentoring Relationship. Student-athletes have built-in adult mentors found in their coaches, administrators, and staff as well as peer mentors in their teams. MSL research (Campbell, Smith, Dugan, & Komives, 2012; Dugan et al., 2013) found that fostering high-quality mentoring opportunities was related to high levels of leadership capacity. Because of the time spent together and the common goal of winning shared among teammates and coaches, mentorship can develop easier than in many other student groups. Athletic mentoring (whether it comes from a teammate or a coach) is a natural fit for a team and should be developed using a structured mentoring program. Schools should encourage and develop good mentors, including coaches and teammates. However, schools should also identify mentors across campus.

There are a number of important people in the life of a student-athlete, each with the potential to influence and develop the leadership characteristics of a student-athlete. Through formal and informal practices, these individuals have the ability to influence the student-athlete and unleash his or her leadership potential. Kouzes and Posner (2006) say "the leaders who have the most influence on us are those who are closest to us" (p. 35). Although peer mentoring can be vital, this chapter focuses on the role administrators and coaches can have as a mentor.

Advisor, Counselor, or Academic Coordinator.   First, the role of the advisor, counselor, or academic coordinator is often on the front lines of knowing the students personally. The advisor knows an athlete's long-term academic and career goals. Academic advisors need to be knowledgeable of leadership training programs that focus on skills and development to help connect athletes to these programs. For example, the NCAA Leadership Forum, APPLE Conference, or Career in Sport Forum, each focuses on tangible self-leadership development by using assessments such as StrengthsFinder, DiSC assessment, or True Colors, which help students understand their own styles and how to integrate with others.

Athletics Administrators.   In addition to academic advisors, other administrators within the athletic department can play a role in helping student-athletes grow in their own leadership traits. For instance, at Georgia Tech, Theresa Wenzel, associate athletic director & senior woman administrator, believes that administrators should be active in encouraging leadership development.

> Athletic administrators have a responsibility to not only mentor coaches but also student-athletes. Any good leader in college athletics should make it a priority to teach student-athletes how to be intentional and strategic in defining and developing their core values through conversations and programs about daily decision making and life choices. (T. Wenzel, personal communication, November 12, 2014)

Coaches.   Finally, it seems obvious that coaches have the potential for the greatest influence in the development of student-athletes; however, not all coaches are good leaders. Just as the players have different styles, so, too, do the coaches. Coaches bring to the table different leadership styles. Each coach develops their own leadership style through years of experience and the influence of others (Sullivan & Kent, 2010; Vallée & Bloom, 2005). In turn, they must do the same for their student-athletes. From a student-development perspective, there is a duty and obligation to foster the development of student-athletes through their sport experience, while working towards athletic achievement. Establishing a supportive environment that empowers student-athletes to develop as leaders is necessary. Specifically, coaches can develop students in a number of practical ways.

- A coach can encourage students to take advantage of leadership opportunities within athletics and on campus. Dugan and Komives (2006) recommend that leadership be connected "to other social identities so students can explore their leadership practices and personal leadership identity" (p. 19).
- Coaches can focus on player self-leadership development. It is important to "support students in adopting an accurate and healthy self-awareness regarding their leadership capacity. This involves helping students to better align their lives of self-efficacy for leadership with actual knowledge and skills" (Dugan & Komives, 2006, p. 19). It is essential that a student-athlete gain self-awareness before leading others.
- Leadership development assessments, including personal assessments such as Myers-Briggs and others previously mentioned, can help students gain insight into their own styles of leading and communicating. The role of student-athletes is such that sometimes, they are leaders and at other times they are followers. This should be developed to improve one's own understanding.
- In the team captain role, a coach can mentor the student-athlete on a regular basis to help them talk through problems, not always resolving the problems for them, but rather helping them navigate finding their own solution.
- A coach can also make a concerted effort to identify leaders even when they are not the best athletes. These individuals who are not the most athletically talented might have more interest in helping the team in other ways, including team building opportunities and peer mentoring.
- Coaches have a responsibility to continually develop themselves so they may be a better example for their students. Taking advantage of campus opportunities, personal reflections, or national training such as Nike's Villa 7, the National Association of Collegiate Women Athletics Administrators (NACWA) Leadership Symposium, or the NCAA Leadership Institute can help make a difference in the example each coach sets for his or her team. Established leaders, such as head coaches, have a responsibility to model humility and be lifelong learners, committed to growing and being better leaders.

Athletic Departments.   Administrative support from the athletic department is key to developing leadership programs that help student-athletes grow. This buy-in also comes with financial resources for programmatic initiatives. Without programs, efforts, and training, student-athletes are reliant on what is available at their institution, which will often conflict with their athletic commitments. Having opportunities that are specific to the student-athlete will help them develop leadership skills that affect both team and personal growth. When financial resources from the athletic department are not available, there must remain a commitment for collaborations within the campus to support the effort.

In addition, athletic departments need to increase their assessment efforts. Although assessment is addressed in greater detail in Chapter 9, athletic departments should continuously evaluate their leadership development programs. In an era of accountability and a commitment to learning outcomes in higher education, assessing that student-athletes are actually learning and developing leadership skills are essential.

Some universities have established additional leadership programs beyond athletic competition that focus on other areas of college life, such as academic progress and social development. Student-athletes have mentors, in both faculty and administrator roles, who provide support for leadership skills not specifically related to their sport. For example, at Washington and Lee, a Division III school in Lexington, Virginia, administrators have extended their mentorship of student-athletes to include faculty as mentors. The Faculty Athletic Mentor program at Washington and Lee is a formalized support program for student-athletes designed to be more intentional with their mentoring (Washington and Lee University, 2014).

Challenges That Impede Leadership Development

Although opportunities exist for leadership development programs to flourish in intercollegiate athletic departments, there are challenges that impede progress. Student-athletes have high demands placed on their time, as they are often trying to juggle the academic load with the commitment of being an athlete. Research has shown that student-athletes spend between 30 and 40 hours per week on their sport (Pope, 2009).

The lack of time leads to numerous scheduling conflicts and forces student-athletes to limit their involvement in other activities, including leadership programs that are not able to accommodate their narrow availability. Leadership programs designed for traditional students are likely to be ineffective for a typical student-athlete because of the student-athletes' lack of attendance. Thus, it is important to develop experiential learning opportunities that focus on leadership development while the athlete is participating in their sport.

Lack of involvement in other programs such as student government, recreational sports, residence life, Greek life, or weekend programming can

create misunderstandings and even animosity on campus. University con-
stituents may perceive athletes as apathetic toward other endeavors when,
in fact, many student-athletes just do not have the time to get involved
in other programs. Students, faculty, and administrators not aware of the
typical student-athlete schedule may develop negative biases toward the
student-athlete. It is not uncommon for student-athletes to be labeled as
unconcerned about academic work or other extracurricular opportunities
(Baucom & Lantz, 2001; Comeaux, 2011).

Research suggests that leadership development works best when implemented in a supportive environment, which for college sports teams is established by the head coach (Evans, Forney, Guido, Patton, & Renn, 2010).
The head coach in college athletics establishes rules and develops a protocol
for how the team will perform specific tasks. Coaches, for better or worse,
will establish an environment where they develop the motivation to embrace the process of how to become a leader. Those coaches who embrace
leadership development, encourage their team to develop key skills, and
obtain sufficient experience to learn how to lead may be the most effective
(Voight, 2012).

However, the reality is that coaches are not hired to implement leadership development programs: they are paid to win. An effective leadership
development program requires resources that many coaches feel are better
spent elsewhere. Leadership development is a lengthy process that requires
coaches to obtain leadership development knowledge, find the time to integrate leadership training, encourage learning, and find ways to evaluate
the success of what has been done. This, along with the pressures to produce immediate results, makes leadership in sport very complex (Vidic &
Burton, 2011).

Regardless, coaches should identify ways to give leadership responsibilities to student-athletes beyond the formal role of captain. Even sport-
specific summer camps can briefly allow student-athletes to serve as
counselor or coach and lead young people. Providing leadership opportunities during practices, off-season workouts, community outreach programs,
team meetings, or even game situations should not be given only to captains
or designated leaders. Anderson's (2012) study demonstrated that students
who participate in sport have higher levels of self-efficacy than students
who do not participate in sport. This provides coaches and mentors an opportunity to be more intentional in creating programs that develop student-
athletes' leadership capacity by connecting to existing leadership models.

Current Leadership Initiatives

On a national level, the NCAA has a number of programs for student-
athletes in any division. Most often these programs are at little or no
expense to the institution. The NCAA Student-Athlete Leadership Forum helps student-athletes improve communication, assess behavioral and

communication styles, gain an appreciation for diversity, and clarify their values (NCAA, n.d.). The Student Athlete Advisory Council (SAAC) exists at both campus and national levels. In this case, being a member of SAAC allows a student-athlete to work across sport to achieve goals. NCAA leadership initiatives and SAAC are directly aligned; they both promote opportunities that will enhance the student-athlete experience.

There are a few unique student-athlete leadership programs already taking place on campus. At Marquette University, the intercollegiate athletics department partnered with an already existing campus leadership program, Students Taking Active Roles (STAR). The program's mission is to develop, challenge, and expand new students' understanding of leadership. Through this program, students are able to define their personal leadership style, demonstrate a respect for differences, and communicate the skills and talents they have to create change in themselves and others (J. Dooley, personal communication, July 1, 2013). Recognizing that the greatest conflict for student-athletes is their schedule, a special section of this program was created that met four times each semester, rather than in one academic term, accommodating athletes' extensive travel schedules. This program takes a foundational approach of developing first-year, or freshman, students before they are put into leadership roles.

Another well-established program focused on student-athlete leadership and spanning the years of an athlete's career is at Duke University. Duke's ACTION Program includes upper division student-athletes who serve as mentors and facilitators through a curriculum that addresses teamwork, leadership, and transition skills. In addition, Duke's sophomores participate in the S.O.L.E. (Sophomore Outdoor Leadership Experience) program, which includes team and individual challenge activities. Duke also includes an Advancing Leaders program that "prepares juniors to take on future leadership roles within their teams" (Duke University, 2014, para. 4).

Leadership development programs are not just found at the major Division I level. Schools at the mid-major level of Division I or at Division II or III schools have also found it important to establish formal and informal programs focused on leadership. In some cases, schools have worked with private companies to establish leadership programs and in other cases, schools have used the campus community to help birth grassroots leadership development opportunities. Both outside private firms that specialize in leadership development or using university resources can be successful; regardless of who is running the program, the athletic department must be supportive of a program grounded in college student development.

Conclusion

Effective leadership development takes time and collaboration. It is recommended that any leadership program for student-athletes be established and supported at the administrative level, whether it be athletic administration, student life, or a combination of administrators and staff. Due to the nature of the industry, it is not uncommon for coaches to leave, so therefore it is best to have the program run through an office not directly connected to one team or coach to maintain continuity.

Research supports the idea that college athletics is an ideal lab for fostering leadership growth. The approach must be collaborative, intentional, and comprehensive to truly develop student-athletes who can effectively lead themselves and their teams. The ultimate goal in establishing leadership programs in the intercollegiate athletic landscape is for students to gain skills that transfer far beyond their years as a student-athlete.

References

Anderson, M. (2012). *The leader development of college students who participate in different levels of sport.* Unpublished doctoral dissertation, The Ohio State University, Columbus. Retrieved from https://etd.ohiolink.edu/!etd.send_file?accession=osu1339154225&disposition=inline

Baucom, C., & Lantz, C. (2001). Faculty attitudes toward male Division II student-athletes. *Journal of Sport Behavior, 24,* 265–276.

Brown, T. N., Jackson, J. S., Brown, K. T., Sellers, R. M., Keiper, S., & Manuel, W. J. (2003). "There's no race on the playing field": Perceptions of racial discrimination among White and Black athletes. *Journal of Sport and Social Issues, 27,* 162–183.

Campbell, C. M., Smith, M., Dugan, J. P., & Komives, S. R. (2012). Mentors and college student leadership outcomes: The importance of position and process. *Review of Higher Education, 35*(4), 595–625.

Comeaux, E. (2011). A study of attitudes toward college student-athletes: Implications for faculty-athletics engagement. *The Journal of Negro Education, 80*(4), 521–532.

Cunningham, G. (2007). *Diversity in sport organizations.* Scottsdale, AZ: Holcomb Hathaway, Publishers.

Day, D., Sin, H., & Chen, T. (2004). Assessing the burdens of leadership: Effects of formal leadership roles on individual performance over time. *Personnel Psychology, 57,* 573–605.

Dugan, J., & Komives, S. (2006). *Developing leadership capacity in college students: Findings from a national study.* College Park, MD: National Clearinghouse of Leadership Programs. Retrieved from https://nclp.umd.edu/include/pdfs/MSLReport-FINAL.pdf

Dugan, J. P., Kodama, C., Correia, B., & Associates (2013). *Multi-Institutional Study of Leadership insight report: Leadership program delivery.* College Park, MD: National Clearinghouse for Leadership Programs.

Duke University. (2014). *Duke athletic leadership program.* Retrieved from http://www.goduke.com/ViewArticle.dbml?ATCLID=3656936

Dupuis, M., Bloom, G. A., & Loughead, T. M. (2006). Team captains' perceptions of athlete leadership. *Journal of Sport Behavior, 29*(1), 60–78.

Evans, N. J., Forney, D. S., Guido, F. M., Patton, L. D., & Renn, K. A. (2010). *Student development in college: Theory, research, and practice* (2nd ed.). San Francisco, CA: John Wiley & Sons.

Kouzes, J. M., & Posner, B. Z. (2006). *The leadership challenge* (4th ed.). San Francisco, CA: Jossey-Bass.

Lowney, C. (2003). *Heroic leadership.* Chicago, IL: Loyola Press.

NCAA. (n.d.). *Student-athlete leadership forum.* Retrieved from http://www.ncaa.org/about/resources/leadership-development-programs-and-resources/student-athlete-leadership-forum

Pope, J. (2009, September 4). NCAA athletes working long hours, survey says. *Diverse Education*. Retrieved from http://diverseeducation.com/article/13021/

Sitkin, S., & Hackman, J. R. (2011). Developing team leadership: An interview with coach Mike Krzyzewski. *Academy of Management Learning & Education, 10*, 394–501.

Sullivan, P., & Kent, A. (2010). Coaching efficacy as a predictor of leadership style in intercollegiate athletics. *Journal of Applied Sport Psychology, 15*(1), 1–11.

University of Wisconsin. (2014). *Diversity and inclusion program*. Retrieved from http://www.uwbadgers.com/diversity/

Vallée, C. N., & Bloom, G. A. (2005). Building a successful university program: Key and common elements of expert coaches. *Journal of Applied Sport Psychology, 17*(3), 179–196.

Vidic, Z., & Burton, D. (2011). Developing effective leaders: Motivational correlates of leadership styles. *Journal of Applied Sport Psychology, 23*, 277–291.

Voight, M. (2012). A leadership development intervention program: A case study with two elite teams. *The Sports Psychologist, 26*, 604–623.

Washington and Lee University. (2014). *Faculty mentors for Washington and Lee Athletics teams*. Retrieved from http://www.generalssports.com/information/Inside_Athletics /Faculty_mentors/fac_men

Yukelson, D., Weinberg, R., Jackson, A., & Richardson, P. (1983). Interpersonal attraction and leadership in interactive collegiate sport teams. *Journal of Sport Behavior, 6*(1), 28–36.

ANTHONY WEAVER is an associate professor in Sport and Event Management in the School of Communications at Elon University.

KATHLEEN SIMET is a learning specialist in academic support in the Department of Athletics at Marquette University.

Collegiate recreation student employment opportunities are found in such areas as facilities, intramurals, aquatics, fitness, and outdoor adventure. Recreation is one of the largest providers of student employment opportunities on campuses across the country with an important role in student employee leadership development.

6

Collegiate Recreation Student Employee as Student Leader

Cara W. McFadden, Julia Wallace Carr

There is a growing body of research assisting practitioners in understanding the connection between student employment and college student development (Astin, 1984; Salisbury, Pascarella, Padgett, & Blaich, 2012). In addition, there is research focused directly on college students working in collegiate recreation environments (Hall, 2013; Johnson, Kaiser, & Bell, 2012; Kellison & James; 2011; Miller & Grayson, 2006; Wallace Carr, 2005) as well as literature on student employment and leadership development (Luzzo, 1999; Perozzi, 2009).

Departments across campus are accountable for illustrating relevance and effectiveness by providing learning opportunities for students in the work environment. A constructive focal point for practitioners is to intentionally develop leadership capacity of student employees. This chapter briefly reviews the differing collegiate recreation environments, the development of student employees, key variables of student employment, and the development of leadership capacity through student employment. Finally, the role of the student employee is discussed and sustainable approaches are shared.

Collegiate Recreation

The role of collegiate recreation on campuses evolved from its foundation of intramural sports to a profession that believes in holistic wellness and lifelong activity. The purpose of collegiate recreation is wellness and learning within the university environment (Hardin, 2013). Collegiate recreation

New Directions for Student Leadership, no. 147, Fall 2015 © 2015 Wiley Periodicals, Inc., A Wiley Company
Published online in Wiley Online Library (wileyonlinelibrary.com) • DOI: 10.1002/yd.20144

departments vary in the number of staff used to operate facilities and provide programs, and typically will report to either student life or athletics.

The majority of positions in collegiate recreation departments are filled
by student employees (Mull, Bayless, & Jamieson, 2005). For example at
Elon University (n.d.), a small private university of 6,483 students, there
are three full-time employees and 140 student employees (D. Norris, personal communication, November 12, 2014); at James Madison University
(2014), a public institution of 20,181 students, a total of 24 full-time employees, 9 graduate assistants, and 400 student employees (J. Wallace Carr,
personal communication, November 12, 2014); and at the Ohio State University (2013), a large public research institution of 63,964 students, a total
of 60 full-time employees, 14 graduate assistants, and 950 student employees (D. Stenta, personal communication, November 12, 2014).

Collegiate recreation departments are a prime location on campus for
student leadership development of college students by providing an environment to study a large number of student employees in a unique setting
(Hall, 2013). As practitioners, it is necessary to know that there is not one
leadership program, training, or initiative that fits all. Those responsible
for creating plans to develop student employee leadership capacity must
discern the relationship between the components that make up their collegiate recreation environment; number of programmatic areas, size of department (i.e., number of facilities, programs, total students employed), and
their responsibility as a supervisor of student employees.

Developing Student Employees' Leadership Capacity Using Chickering's Seven Vectors

In 1969, Chickering published *Education and Identity* that built off Erikson's
research (stages of identity and intimacy development). From his work, he
found identity to be at the core of college student development. Once a
student established identity, he or she can then progress through other developmental stages. As introduced in Chapter 4, through the examination of
developmental stages, Chickering identified seven vectors of development,
which were then revised by Chickering and Reisser (1993) to include the
following: (a) developing competence, (b) managing emotions, (c) moving
through autonomy toward independence, (d) developing mature interpersonal relationships, (e) establishing identity, (f) developing purpose, and
(g) developing integrity. With the seven vectors in mind Chickering and
Reisser (1993) also noted that there are powerful influences in the university setting that can influence student development. These factors include
(a) institutional objectives, (b) institutional size, (c) student–faculty relationships, (d) curriculum, (e) teaching, (f) friendships and student communities, and (g) student development programs and services (Chickering
& Reisser, 1993; Wallace Carr, 2013).

Understanding how college students develop during their time at the university is vital in providing opportunities for student employees to develop their leadership capacity. Students have reported that working in collegiate recreation assisted them in learning academic content, learning about others and recognizing difference, and gaining skills for their career, such as leadership skills and building relationships (Hall, 2013). Student employees' responsibility in the collegiate recreation setting is vital for the department to fully function.

Role of Student Employee.   Student employees play a critical role in the collegiate recreation setting from ensuring safety of participants, providing excellent customer service, facilitating successful programs, leading adventure activities and trips, instructing group fitness classes, officiating intramural sports, or serving as president of a sport club. Many colleges and universities count on students, usually ranging in age from 18 to 25, to make up a large portion of their part-time workforce. Studies of student involvement in higher education indicate that students are less involved in traditional campus activities and are more involved in activities such as academic clubs, service learning, community service, and work (Kuh, Palmer, & Kish, 2003).

This higher level of involvement of students in the on-campus work environment has created new challenges for higher education administrators and educators. They must deal with not only the differences in age and the various developmental stages of student participants but also with those of the students they supervise as employees. The differences are also functional in nature and are primarily in work arrangements: part-time and full-time professional positions, graduate assistant positions and part-time undergraduate student wage, and work–study positions, but they also include the workplace learning needs of each constituency group. The result is a greater challenge for an organization due to the blending of student and professional staff members to provide high-quality service to patrons and to meet the institutional and departmental mission and goals. Supervisors in these settings want students to have responsibility. However, it is imperative for supervisors to be patient and to understand the quality of service may falter as the student experiences growth during their employment while developing their leadership capacity.

Increasing the challenge for administrators is an expectation of providing a workplace experience that is meaningful, has purpose, and supports a wide variety of employee learning and developmental needs. All involved—administrators, supervisors, and coworkers—must understand that each group, from full-time professionals to undergraduate student employees and all of those in between, may be looking for something different from their employment experience or have a different perspective about what will add value to their time with the organization. A meaningful learning experience for one group may not generate the same reaction from another, due to the vast generational and developmental differences present in one workplace (Wallace Carr, 2005).

Variables of Student Employment. In 1996, Chickering, Frank, and Robinson (1996) suggested a conceptual framework concerning relationships among learning styles, employment settings, and student–employer roles that are most stage appropriate. The framework shares that there is a relationship between five components: (a) ego development, (b) motive for work, (c) type of work setting, (d) job characteristics, and (e) employer (supervisor role). Understanding the complexity of the campus recreation work environment and variables related to the student employee experience highlights the complexity in the development of one student's leadership capacity within the workplace. Supervisors must be aware of student growth stages and the employer's stated needs to create an environment that encourages learning and preparation for students to develop their full leadership capacity.

To better understand the development of the student in an employee role, it is necessary to determine how college students perceive and describe their learning experiences during participation in an on-campus employment experience. Wallace Carr (2005) conducted a case study of student employees at a campus recreation center. The purpose of the study was to explore the learning that occurs during the on-campus employment experience from the perspective of the college student. The results indicated that students perceive and describe their learning experiences and avenues for development from three different lenses: informal learning (Marsick & Watkins, 1990), skill development, and work environment.

Informal learning consisted of dialogue with their peers (students on the same level of employment), student supervisors, and professional staff supervisors; performance management through evaluations, informal conversations, coaching sessions; and teachable moments with supervisors, and incidental learning was described as learning from mistakes and by doing. Skill development included people skills, transferrable skills, and workplace skills. Finally, the workplace environment affected learning as well. It was determined that learning took place when the workplace was fun, the student could work autonomously, student development was stressed, and teamwork was emphasized. McFadden, Skaggs, and Janosik (2013) validated an instrument to measure the development of college students' sense of competence (confidence in their own ability), Chickering's (1969; Chickering & Reisser, 1993) first vector. The *Sense of Competence Scale-Revised (SCS-R)* is focused on developing intellectual, interpersonal, and physical skills. The instrument relates to the three learning frames by providing one way to understand students' competence to assist administrators in the modification of the institution's academic and social environment to enhance the development of students. Identifying the links between a student's sense of competence can assist administrators in determining student's readiness to take on different roles within the work environment.

A 2009 study shared the theoretical foundation for the type of work experience and provides examples of practice (Perozzi, 2009). Formal training (Eraut, 2000), new employee orientation, tutorials in job tasks, and retreats are listed examples (Perozzi, 2009). Other experiences listed include (a) informal training, (b) observation of coworkers, (c) collaboration and teamwork, (d) feedback from peers, (e) feedback from supervisor, (f) informal interactions with supervisor, (g) task repetition, (h) problem solving, (i) idea experimentation, (j) reflection, (k) intuitive decision making, and (l) congruence between job and coursework or career path (Perozzi, 2009). The purpose of the study was to understand the learning that takes place across varying student employee positions to be proactive in regard to student development. One of the organizational implications found there was a deficit in job descriptions and suggested the development of learning-focused job descriptions. These descriptions would include general duties, connect to learning outcomes, and list the student employee program philosophy at the beginning of the job description (Lewis & Contreras, 2009). This can then be applied to the creation of the collegiate recreation job descriptions by clearly identifying the leadership learning outcomes.

Understanding student learning styles, student development, and types of work experience are imperative in creating intentional experiences to develop students' leadership capacity. These concepts support the role of the Leadership Identity Development model (Komives, Longerbeam, Owen, Mainella, & Osteen, 2006) in this unique environment discussed in Chapter 3. Within a collegiate recreation setting, it is crucial for supervisors to accept the idea that students have differing learning styles and are exposed to varying learning experiences during their time at work.

Supervision and Student Leadership Positions. This section focuses on supervising student employees and practical tools that administrators can use for developing the on-campus job to ensure that it goes beyond workplace tasks and creates an out-of-classroom practical learning and work experience for the students. Supervisors can conduct a job analysis with an added step of creating a process for a developmental performance progression for positions within their area of responsibility. Sample job titles are included in Table 6.1. The leaders of the organization must conduct a strategic planning process for student employment positions if a student development orientation is pervasive in the organization. In the strategic planning process, a great deal of intentionality is given to job classifications and titles to ensure that the same type of developmental and leadership progression takes place in all areas of the organization.

Job Analysis.   The job analysis refers to the activity of determining the job description and specifications of the position (Lussier, 2011). The job description provides tasks and responsibilities of a position. The job specifications are the qualifications of the person who will fill the position. These include certifications, education level, and the knowledge, skills, and abilities required of the position.

Table 6.1   Supervision and Student Leadership Positions

Job Classifications

Assistants	Entry level, no previous training required: 8–12 hours per week
Specialists	Requires previous training, experience, or certification: 10–14 hours per week
Managers	Leadership of assistants required, perform management tasks: 10–14 hours per week
Supervisors	Part of organizations leadership team, oversees entire facility: 14–16 hours per week

Student Employee Classifications and Job Titles

Assistant	Equipment Maintenance Assistant, Fiscal Tech Assistant, Fitness Assistant, Group Fitness Assistant, Maintenance Assistant, Marketing Assistant, Member Service Assistant, Office Services Assistant, Officials (noncertified), Payroll & Reservation Assistant, Recreation Assistant, Scorekeeper, Special Event Assistant
Specialist	Adventure Team Empowerment With Adventure for Madison (TEAM) Facilitator, Climbing Wall Specialist, Fitness Instructor, Group Fitness Instructor, Lifeguard, Maintenance Specialist, Marketing Specialist, Member Service Specialist, Office Services Specialist, Officials (certified)
Manager	Adventure Manager, Adventure Lead TEAM Facilitator, Fitness Manager, Group Fitness Manager, Emergency Medical Technician Manager (Head EMT), Lifeguard Manager (Head Lifeguard), Informal Recreation Manager, Intramural Site Manager, Maintenance Manager, Member Service Manager, Nutrition Manager, Office Services Manager, Personal Trainer Manager, Special Event Manager, Sport Club Executive, Sport Club Fiscal Assistant, Technology Manager, Wellness Manager
Supervisor	Operations Supervisor, Special Event Supervisor

Source: Wallace Carr, J., Nettesheim, M., & Nickel, E. (1995). *Supervision and student leadership positions*. Harrisonburg, VA: University Recreation, James Madison University.

Developmental Performance Sequence.   Following a thorough job analysis for all the positions within a respective area of responsibility such as fitness, intramurals, or member services for example, the supervisor would focus on student development and identify behaviors for the specific position that are developmental in nature. Supervisors focus on specific behaviors that can be identified and observed that are related to a position and then create a sequence of performance that relates to a developmental progression within an organization based on observable behaviors (see Table 6.2).

Along with the information presented in the job analysis and developmental performance sequences, supervisors need to understand and educate their employees on the concepts of leadership roles in order for them to get the most out of their work experience. Komives, Lucas, and McMahon (2013) identify three roles that can be observed in a campus recreation facility: positional leaders, leaders and followers, or participants. Many students assume that they cannot move forward if they are not in a positional leadership position. The information shared by Komives and her

Table 6.2   Developmental Performance Sequence

Developmental Period	Timing	Behavioral Outcomes
Preperformance	Prior to First Training	The student can articulate: • job description • basic position expectations
Basic Training	Up to First Evaluation or End of First 3 Months of Employment	The student employee can articulate: • the departmental mission • the customer service ethic • basic policies and procedures for their respective area of assignment The student employee can demonstrate: • some of the basic skills required of the position (department would identify most important skills) • greeting customers • adherence of departmental and area policies and procedures
Basic Performer	End of First Year or End of 2 Semesters of Employment	The student employee: • completes tasks described on the job description to a "meets expectations" performance standard • articulates the basic knowledge required of an employee in this position • demonstrates all of the basic skills required of the position • demonstrates seeking out the needs of customers • works independently on assigned intermittent tasks
Blue Chipper	1+ Years of Employment	The student employee: • exceeds the basic expectations presented in the job description • continually asks for more responsibilities • initiates and leads special projects • is a creative problem solver • seeks additional certifications, knowledge, and skills beyond the basic qualifications required by the position • serves as a role model for policy and procedure enforcement and adherence • serves as an on-the-job staff trainer • works independently on projects • strives to exceed customer expectations • may work at the manager level

Table 6.2   Continued

Developmental Period	Timing	Behavioral Outcomes
Shining Star	1+ Years of Employment	The student employee: • works at the highest performance level (excellent) on all basic expectations presented in the job description • demonstrates basic supervisory skills • is self-directed • seeks responsibility • demonstrates the ability to lead and supervise the day-to-day operations of the area • demonstrates all aspects of the organizational customer service ethic • may work at a supervisory level

Source: Nettesheim, M., & Wallace Carr, J. (1996). *Developmental performance sequence*. Harrisonburg, VA: University Recreation, James Madison University.

colleagues (2013) serve to educate university staff that student leaders can be found in any position within the organization.

Positional Leader. A leader can be labeled as a positional leader, meaning the student typically has a title. In the recreation setting, student leaders include volleyball club president, intramural supervisor, facility manager, or aquatics supervisor (these titles vary based on the differing recreational settings). Being in a leadership position does not always mean that the student is a good leader or is respected by peers; typically the student is hired, elected, or appointed to assume a specific responsibility (Komives et al., 2013). This is often experienced in the workplace by professionals, too, where individuals are placed into a position of leadership but are not ready to lead the organization. Understanding that this occurs supports the investment in developing students' leadership capacity. Creating intentionally integrated opportunities to develop students' leadership throughout all the positions within the organization is vital.

Leader. A leader on the other hand is entirely different. It refers to anyone who actively engages with others to make positive change (Komives et al., 2013). The challenging part for practitioners is accurately identifying these student leaders who act with or without a positional title. As a positional leader, group member, or participant, a student leader can emerge by taking initiative and moving a team or group closer to a goal to make positive change.

Follower. In the past, a follower was referred to as a subordinate, employee, or member of a specific group. However, Komives, Lucas, and McMahon (2007) use the term participant to best describe the follower.

Participants are involved in the leadership process, actively sharing leadership with other group members. Participants include the informal and formal positional leader in a group as well as active group members who seek to be involved in a group change. Participants are active, engaged, and intentional. (Komives et al., 2007, p. 18)

There is limited research in the area of developing leadership capacity in the collegiate recreation setting. Administrators are creating intentional experiences in the work environment related to positional leader, leader, and follower experiences. Professionals supervising students in the recreation environment must integrate opportunities for students to exhibit leadership in any three (positional, leader, follower) roles.

Current Practice.   A 2013 study by Tingle, Cooney, Asbury, and Tate addressed the improvement of student leadership capacity as a result of working in collegiate recreation. The study tried to determine if significant differences in leadership development among three differing student employee groups existed based on training received in each group. The researchers created the Student Leadership Retreat Training (SLRT) program (Tingle et al., 2013). Students were divided into three groups: mentors, midlevel supervisors, and new hires. The program lasted a full year and with the completion of the program students would understand components of leadership and mentorship; students in the mentor group would also improve leadership competencies. To measure growth of leadership capacity, Kouzes and Posner's (2006) *Student Leadership Practices Inventory* was used. The study found that by having student participate in a yearlong leadership training program, collegiate recreation professionals can create meaningful leadership programs (Tingle et al., 2013).

At Elon University, each area of collegiate recreation (e.g., intramurals, facilities, group fitness) is led by a team leader (TL). The TLs serve as a student leader for programmatic areas in the collegiate recreation department and assist in the administration of a comprehensive campus recreation program. TLs are responsible for hiring, training, scheduling, and firing of staff within their specific work area. The TLs do represent positional leaders within the organization; however, they are trained by professional staff to develop skills to motivate and empower their team members to accomplish goals by using the Drexel/Sibbet Team Performance Model (Grove Consultants International, n.d.). Programmatic areas include aquatics, club sports, event management, facilities, fitness, group exercise, intramurals, marketing, outdoors, and south campus facilities. Main responsibilities for the TLs include daily programmatic operations and supervision of fellow student employees. The learning outcomes for the TLs are decided annually and are written in an Annual Report of Assessment Progress (ARAP; D. Norris, personal communication, November 12, 2014).

At James Madison University, a Common Training Day is held during August Training Week. Student employees are divided into new hires,

NEW DIRECTIONS FOR STUDENT LEADERSHIP • DOI: 10.1002/yd

veterans, and managers. There are specific learning outcomes for each training group. The individuals who are in the manager sections are basically the positional leaders of the organization. The outcomes for this group center around these leaders being able to teach the concepts, policies, and procedures learned to the new hires during on the job training sessions. In addition to this 1-day training session, the organization has a Student Leadership Series that is optional and provides educational sessions on a wide range of leadership and personal development topics throughout the year.

At the Ohio State University, student employees can participate in the Emerging Leadership Institute (ELI). ELI is a leadership development program geared toward collegiate recreation student employees within Student Life Recreational Sports. The Social Change Model of Leadership Development (HERI, 1996) is the theoretical foundation for ELI. Intentional experiential learning experiences and the institute's curriculum are constructed based on findings within the Multi-Institutional Study of Leadership (MSL; Dugan, Kodama, Correia, & Associates, 2013). Students participate in experiences that are divided into four tenets: personal growth and development, group dynamics, community engagement, and global impact (B. Johnson, personal communication, December 14, 2014).

These examples illustrate that there are opportunities to develop intentional experiences grounded in leadership theory (Dugan & Komives, 2011) and student development theory (Owen, 2012) for students in the collegiate recreation to develop leadership capacity in a setting that can take place beyond training for the actual role the student has as an employee. Clearly, the size of the institution as well as the makeup of the professional staff and student employees does not hinder integrating well-planned initiatives to develop students' leadership capacity as a student employee working in collegiate recreation.

Conclusion

Collegiate recreation professionals know they influence the development of student employees. Being housed in the higher education environment, every professional working in collegiate recreation is responsible for the development of students. If collegiate recreation staff members believe in developing student leaders, then they must create intentional learning experiences for students to have an opportunity to grow within the collegiate recreation setting by linking their identity to developing their personal leadership capacity.

References

Astin, A. W. (1984). Student involvement: A developmental theory for higher education. *Journal of College Student Personnel, 25,* 297–308.
Chickering, A. (1969). *Education and identity.* San Francisco, CA: Jossey-Bass.

Chickering, A., & Reisser, L. (1993). *Education and identity* (2nd ed.). San Francisco, CA: Jossey-Bass.

Chickering, A. W., Frank, I., & Robinson, V. (1996). Encouraging student development through student employment. In R. Kincaid (Ed.), *Student employment: Linking college and the workplace* (pp. 11–24). University of South Carolina, SC: National Resource Center for the Freshman Year Experience and Students in Transition.

Dugan, J. P., Kodama, C., Correia, B., & Associates (2013). *Multi-Institutional Study of Leadership insight report: Leadership program delivery.* College Park, MD: National Clearinghouse for Leadership Programs.

Dugan, J. P., & Komives, S. R. (2011). Leadership theories. In S. R. Komives, J. P. Dugan, J. E. Owen, C. Slack, & W. Wagner (Eds.), *The handbook for student leadership development* (pp. 35–57). San Francisco, CA: Jossey-Bass.

Elon University. (n.d.). *About Elon University.* Retrieved from http://www.elon.edu /e-web/about/default.xhtml

Eraut, M. (2000). Non-formal learning and tacit knowledge in professional work. *British Journal of Educational Psychology, 70,* 113–136.

Grove Consultants International (n.d.). Drexler/Sibbet team performance model. Retrived from http://www.grove.com/site/ourwk_gm_tp.html

Hall, S. L. (2013). Influence of campus recreation employment on student learning. *Recreational Sports Journal, 37*(2), 136–146.

Hardin, S. E. (2013). A career in campus recreational sports. In NIRSA Leaders in Collegiate Recreation, *Campus recreational sports: Managing employees, programs, facilities, and services* (pp. 25–44). Champaign, IL: Human Kinetics.

Higher Education Research Institute [HERI]. (1996). *A social change model of leadership development: Guidebook Version III.* College Park, MD: National Clearinghouse for Leadership Programs.

James Madison University. (2014). *Factsheet.* Retrieved from https://www.jmu.edu/about /fact-and-figures.shtml

Johnson, J. E., Kaiser, A. N., & Bell, R. J. (2012). An examination of variables related to student employment in campus recreation programs. *Recreational Sports Journal, 36*(2), 78–90.

Kellison, T. B., & James, J. D. (2011). Factors influencing job satisfaction of student employees of a recreational sports department at a large, four-year public institution: A case study. *Recreational Sports Journal, 35*(1), 35–44.

Komives, S. R., Longerbeam, S. D., Owen, J. E., Mainella, F. C., & Osteen, L. (2006). A leadership identity development model: Applications from a grounded theory. *Journal of College Student Development, 47,* 401–420.

Komives, S. R., Lucas, N., & McMahon, T. R. (2007). *Exploring leadership: For college students who want to make a difference* (2nd ed.). San Francisco, CA: Jossey-Bass.

Komives, S. R., Lucas, N., & McMahon, T. R. (2013). *Exploring leadership: For college students who want to make a difference* (3rd ed.). San Francisco, CA: Jossey-Bass.

Kuh, G. D., Palmer, M., & Kish, K. (2003). The value of educational purposeful out-of-class experiences. In T. L. Skipper & R. Argo (Eds.), *Involvement in campus activities and the retention of first year college students* (pp. 1–18). Columbia, SC: University of South Carolina.

Lewis, J. S., & Contreras, S. (2009). Student learning outcomes: Empirical research as the bridge between theory and practice. In B. Perozzi (Ed.), *Enhancing student learning through college employment.* Bloomington, IN: Association of College Unions International.

Lussier, R. (2011). *Management fundamentals: Concepts, applications, skill development.* Mason, OH: Cengage Learning.

Luzzo, D. A. (1999). Enhancing students' leadership development: Realizing the benefits of college student employment. *Concepts & Connections: Leadership Opportunities in Student Employment, 7*(2), 1–4.

Marsick, V. J., & Watkins, K. E. (1990). *Informal and incidental learning in the workplace*. London, England: Routledge.

McFadden, C., Skaggs, G., & Janosik, S. (2013). Development and validation of the sense of competence scale-revised. *Journal of Applied Measurement, 14*, 318–331.

Miller, G. L., & Grayson, T. E. (2006). Student employees and recreational sports administrators: A comparison of perceptions. *Recreational Sports Journal, 30*(1), 53–69.

Mull, R. F., Bayless, K. G., & Jamieson, L. M. (2005). *Recreational sport management* (4th ed.). Champaign, IL: Human Kinetics.

Nettesheim, M., & Wallace, J. C. (1996). *Developmental performance sequence*. Harrisonburg, VA: University Recreation, James Madison University

Ohio State University. (2013). *Statistical summary*. Retrieved from http://www.osu.edu /about/default.xhtml

Owen, J. (2012). Using student development theories as conceptual frameworks. In K. L. Guthrie & L. Osteen (Eds.), *New Directions for Student Services No. 140: Developing Students' Leadership Capacity* (pp. 17–33). San Francisco, CA: Jossey-Bass.

Perozzi, B. (2009). *Enhancing student learning through college employment*. Bloomington, IN: Association of College Unions International.

Salisbury, M. H., Pascarella, E. T., Padgett, R. D., & Blaich, C. (2012). The effects of work on leadership development among first-year college students. *Journal of College Student Development, 53*, 300–324.

Tingle, J. K., Cooney, C., Asbury, S. E., & Tate, S. (2013). Developing a student leadership program: The importance of evaluating effectiveness. *Recreational Sports Journal, 37*(1), 2–13.

Wallace Carr, J. (2005). *An exploration of how learning and development emerge for student employees during the on-campus work experience* (Doctoral dissertation). Retrieved from ProQuest Dissertations and Theses. (Accession Order No. 3161580)

Wallace Carr, J. (2013). Program planning using a student learning approach. In NIRSA: Leaders in Collegiate Recreation, *Campus recreational sports: Managing employees, programs, facilities, and services* (pp. 184–196). Champaign, IL: Human Kinetics.

CARA W. MCFADDEN *is an assistant professor in Sport and Event Management in the School of Communications at Elon University.*

JULIA WALLACE CARR *is the senior associate director for University Recreation and is an associate professor in the Department of Sport and Recreation Management, the School of Hospitality, Sport and Recreation Management at James Madison University.*

NEW DIRECTIONS FOR STUDENT LEADERSHIP • DOI: 10.1002/yd

7

This chapter connects concepts and research from positive psychology and leadership studies to support using a strengths-based approach to optimize the leadership development of students involved in recreation and athletics.

Positive Psychology as a Framework for Leadership Development in Recreation and Sport

Amy C. Barnes, James Larcus

For the past 15 years, the growing field of leadership education has seen the creation of leadership models and a new priority for putting research-based theories into practice. During the same time period, the field of positive psychology has gained momentum with its emphasis on personal well-being, constructs like hope and optimism, and a strengths-based focus for individual and group development. In the study of sport, positive psychology frequently appears in research about resilience, optimism, and "flow," which is described as an immersive experience where individuals participate in tasks requiring high levels of challenge and skill as they relate to performance and success (Csikszentmihalyi, 1990). The purpose of this chapter is to introduce the impact positive psychology has made in both leadership development and sport and how student-athletes and collegiate recreation participants can apply what they are learning through physical activity and team sports to other areas of their lives. Practical applications for coaches, teachers, and administrators on how to create experiences that not only support student wellness but also encourage leadership development for all students will be discussed.

What Is Positive Psychology?

Behavioral science has long been the foundation for educators to understand the growth and development of students beyond just academic success. For the past century, psychology has been a science about healing. It was based in a "disease model" of human functioning and about how

New Directions for Student Leadership, no. 147, Fall 2015 © 2015 Wiley Periodicals, Inc., A Wiley Company
Published online in Wiley Online Library (wileyonlinelibrary.com) • DOI: 10.1002/yd.20145

people survive under conditions of adversity. As the new millennium began, several psychologists sought to establish a branch of the field of psychology called *positive psychology* that focuses on individual fulfillment, what makes life worth living, and the discovery of why some people and communities have an increased capacity to thrive (Gable & Haidt, 2005; Seligman & Csikszentmihalyi, 2000; Seligman, Steen, Park, & Peterson, 2005). "At the individual level, positive psychology is about positive individual traits: the capacity for love and vocation, courage, interpersonal skill, aesthetic sensibility, perseverance, forgiveness, originality, future mindedness, spirituality, high talent, and wisdom" (Seligman & Csikszentmihalyi, 2000, p. 5).

Positive psychology and leadership development connect when leaders use their personal talents and strengths in their work and encourage others to do the same. Leaders who understand that their best work is accomplished when all the elements of their well-being are at a healthy level are not only well balanced but often highly successful and happy (Harter & Rath, 2010).

Positive Psychology and Student Success.   Professionals in student affairs and the fields of collegiate recreation, athletics, and wellness initiatives know and understand the importance of physical well-being and how health can negatively or positively affect a person's overall success (Harter & Rath, 2010). Professionals are poised to make a difference on student growth and development in areas such as resilience building and self-efficacy, two areas that have been shown to have a positive impact on leadership development in students (Dugan, Torrez, & Turman, 2014). Resilience, often seen as a by-product of individual reflection and leadership development, is defined as, "the characteristics that enable one to persist in the midst of adversity and positively cope with stress" (Dugan, Kodama, Correia, & Associates, 2013, p. 27). Positive psychology is a framework and research-based approach that could help guide this work and provides a rationale for creating programs that build a connection between physical health, well-being, resilience, and leadership development.

Leadership Development

Whereas student affairs practitioners have helped students develop leadership skills for years, the field of leadership education has recently become a burgeoning area of research and practice in higher education. Leadership studies as an academic discipline is being recognized at institutions across the country through the creation of leadership studies majors and minors, certificate programs, and tenure-track faculty positions created to support these programs. In response to the growth and development of leadership education for students as a discipline, theory and research have emerged on how to facilitate effective and intentional growth. Models and theories explain the growth and development of student leaders and a few of the most used models include those presented in this sourcebook, specifically the

Leadership Identity Development Model (Komives, Owen, Longerbeam, Mainella, & Osteen, 2005), the Relational Leadership Model (Komives, Lucas, & McMahon, 2013), and the Social Change Model of Leadership Development (Higher Education Research Institute, 1996). Leadership development in students has been shown to enhance self-efficacy, civic engagement, character development, academic performance, and personal development (Komives et al., 2005).

Perhaps the largest body of research on student leadership development is from the Multi-Institutional Study of Leadership (MSL), one of the largest studies of college student leadership to date. According to the MSL website, over 250 institutions have joined the study over the past 8 years garnering participation from over 300,000 students (Dugan et al., 2013). As noted in earlier chapters, the emphasis of the social change model is on the development of individual, group, and community values as the essential elements of leadership development for students with essential components including resilience building and social perspective taking. Having resilience helps students overcome the challenges and stresses that are ever present in everyday life. Resilience allows students to persist amid adversity and is a mitigating factor in the developmental readiness of students to focus on building their own leadership capacities (Dugan et al., 2013).

Leadership Capacity and Sport Participation.   Recreation and athletics departments are important places to develop student and professional leaders because a vast number of opportunities exist for students to exhibit leadership in club sports, intramurals, varsity team sports, and student employment. On some campuses, the number of students who participate in sports and university-sponsored recreational programs far exceeds the number of students who officially participate in school-sponsored leadership development programs. Educators ought to consider the potential impact of meeting students "where they are" and helping them translate the activities and leadership experiences they are having in the sports arena into leadership development opportunities that will benefit them long-term.

Recently, Maiya Anderson (2012) used the MSL conceptual and theoretical frameworks, along with the MSL national data set from 2009, to study the effects of varying levels of sport participation on leadership self-efficacy and socially responsible leadership. In Anderson's (2012) study, sport participation was examined across four domains: intercollegiate competition characterized by participation in the National Collegiate Athletic Association (NCAA), National Association of Intercollegiate Athletics (NAIA), or National Junior College Athletic Association (NJCAA); club athletics often referred to as competitive teams that do not receive the same level of funding that intercollegiate teams receive; intramural sport characterized by competition primarily within the institution; and recreation activity such as informal workouts or pick-up games.

Anderson's (2012) findings highlight that students who participated in any sport garnered higher levels of leadership self-efficacy than students who did not participate in any sport or recreation activity. Furthermore, the results were statistically significant when controlled for background, pre-college variables, as well as involvement in college (Anderson, 2012). If leadership self-efficacy is an outcome of sport participation, imagine what could happen if intentional leadership development learning outcomes were created and programs were linked to existing theories.

In a more recent study using MSL data to explore the links between recreation involvement and leadership development, Dugan et al. (2014) highlighted the importance of mentoring as impactful for student leadership development. In fact, mentorship was a significant factor in the leadership development of athletes in the study. The potential impact that positive mentoring and strengths-based coaching can have on the development of self-efficacy could be significant for students.

Following studies like those conducted by Anderson (2012), educators need to discuss ways to then focus on individual stages of student leadership development through the social change model. Mentorship from coaches, older peers, or administrators can help encourage learning and personal growth. For example, if building resilience is already a benefit of sport and recreation, educators could mentor students to understand how to translate that resilience into other aspects of their educational experience. Because self-efficacy is an outcome of participation in recreational sports and athletics, educators can build on this foundation by providing appropriate challenges to help students apply their skills and knowledge outside of the sport context to leadership development. Last, programs could be established to connect students to service-learning, sociocultural conversations, or off-campus involvement (all high-impact practices identified through MSL research), and this could encourage student growth in both the group and societal domains of the social change model of leadership development (Dugan et al., 2013).

Helping Students Identify Talents and Strengths.   By empowering students to see what good or positive aspects they possess, as well as how to use those talents in new or challenging circumstances, educators can create an opportunity for students to see what they are capable of accomplishing both individually and as a member of a team. Strengths-based development involves three stages: identification of talent, integration into one's self-image, and behavioral change (Clifton & Harter, 2003). Although most people think that a well-rounded approach to personal development is key to growth, positive psychology and strengths-based leadership promote that a focus in areas of strength leads to more engagement, productivity, happiness, and well-being (Rath & Conchie, 2008). The Gallup Organization (2014) created an online assessment to help people identify their personal strengths and promoted the use of the instrument in companies and organizations worldwide. In the StrengthsFinder assessment, 34 talent themes are assessed and individuals are provided results that include their top five most used and naturally occurring behaviors expressed as strengths. The

34 Strengths are categorized into four domains of leadership: executing, influencing, relationship building, and strategic thinking (Rath & Conchie, 2008) so individuals can understand the areas in which they excel through teamwork. These groupings lend themselves to productive and meaningful conversations around individual leadership styles, as well as how individuals work as a team with others. A progressive and comprehensive athletic department or collegiate recreation organization could be guided by this approach and philosophy. And discussing assessments like the Strengths-Finder in athletic team settings can help students see how they use their strengths within sports and in other areas of their lives. Recently, an updated third edition of *Exploring Leadership* (Komives et al., 2013) includes material on positive psychology and comes with a Gallup online access code that allows students to take the StrengthsFinder assessment at no additional cost. This book and facilitator guide are extremely useful to educators who are considering implementing a leadership development program or course.

Another aspect of strengths-based leadership is the knowledge and ability to know when certain behaviors or tasks are not an area of strength. The philosophy behind the strengths-based approach advocates that in these cases, instead of trying to be the best in all aspects of a role, individuals should instead learn to delegate and partner with people who have strengths in areas where they are not as talented. In a recent study focused on teamwork in sports, some of the key intervention strategies for the study included finding complementary partners who had strengths in other areas and the use of personal strengths to overcome obstacles or challenges (Gordon, 2012). These two practices allowed coaches to think about players in roles that harnessed their natural strengths in a way that was more intentional and more meaningful for the players and the team as a whole (Gordon, 2012). For example, players identified their strengths within the sport of cricket (e.g., batting) and dedicated their time and energy to training more in those areas of expertise while allowing their teammates to focus in other areas of the game (e.g., fielding; Gordon, 2012). Similarly, an example could include a 7-foot basketball center focusing his/her time and energy on footwork, moves, and shots around the basket compared to letting a guard practice their three-point jump shot. The idea is that with the combination of these skills, talents, and strengths, the overall team functions at a higher level and with more individual success and happiness than if these players focused on an area of weakness.

Gordon (2012) also parallels the positive sport coaching culture of Waters, Scholes, and White (2011) by emphasizing that strengths can be used to build mental toughness, resilience, better team dynamics, and positive results. Similarly, research on leaders of companies and organizations worldwide by the Gallup organization discovered that the most successful leaders spend most of their time in areas of strength, have learned to delegate or partner with others in areas that are not their own strength, use their personal strengths to overcome obstacles in their daily lives, and find new ways of capitalizing on their strengths in new situations or contexts (Rath & Conchie, 2008).

VIA Character Strengths.   Another useful tool, created from early research on positive psychology by Martin Seligman, is the VIA (Virtues in Action) character strength assessment. This assessment, which is free to take online at http://viame.org, highlights core virtues or values that students possess and exhibit as they mature. The VIA is a great way to foster self-awareness for students and to help motivate students through increased awareness of personal character strengths. For example, some of the strengths the assessment measures include hope, perseverance, love of learning, curiosity, kindness, and zest. An individual player on a team who has perseverance as a top strength is going to approach practice from a much different perspective than a player with a love of learning. Coaches can use this information to help guide and improve a player's performance while also encouraging positive leadership development off the field or court. Team captains could participate in leadership training to learn to work more effectively together, and teammates could consider ways that their sport leadership experiences translate to work environments. As the Leadership Identity Development Model (Komives et al., 2005) highlights, students who learn to effectively use their talents within group and team contexts begin to see the value of the contributions that all group members make to the organization and thus learn important aspects of leadership capacity including trust, delegation, and how to encourage the growth of less-experienced peers.

Applying Strengths-Based Leadership Development in Recreational and Athletic Settings

For teachers, coaches, administrators, and supervisors of athletic and collegiate recreation programs, the intersection of leadership development and positive psychology has significant implications for the performative, competitive, and developmental impact sport and recreation have on individuals. Similarly, strengths-based leadership development and positive psychology mirror the 25-year movement of sport psychology (Gould, 2002) and can only be additive, especially when considering the important avenue athletic and recreational sport departments have in terms of leadership development now and in the future.

Collegiate recreation programming, recreation facilities, sport clubs, and athletic departments provide important opportunities for student leadership development because of the sheer number of students who are participating and the work that is already being done to better student health and wellness. As has been evidenced through much of this chapter, translating a focus on personal well-being into a focus on strengths-based leadership development is not a significant change in direction. In fact, the two are closely linked and positive psychology practices can help students both within their sport settings and in other arenas.

The self-awareness gained through leadership development initiatives and the application of positive psychology to areas of growth and success can allow for students to move with more efficacy through their daily stressors. In the recent study using data from the MSL, results indicated there is room to bolster the influence of participation in campus recreation on resilience (Dugan et al., 2014). Resilience building is a key area of student leadership development that campus recreation involvement can foster easily. It may simply be a matter of reminding students of the link between resilience and leadership as well as providing students with knowledge of how positive psychology concepts like resiliency can affect other areas of their lives. Likewise, knowledge of the strengths of others, an appreciative mindset, and learning to partner with others who possess strengths that are different than their own allow for better working teams and groups.

Positive Psychology and Sport Today

The platform for the infusing of strengths and positive psychology into sport and recreation has great potential, and even buy-in, because of its connection and similarities to sport and performance psychology. Gould (2002) notes the call for psychology to move to the optimal functioning parallels exactly what sport psychology has been doing for the past 25 years. Researchers have focused time and energy on how to make athletes great by replicating conditions that support an emphasis on positive outcomes (Gould, 2002).

Positive psychology is being pursued as an effective practice within sport and recreation settings at a variety of levels. From the professional level to high school and college, athletes are being exposed to the principles that enhance their levels of flow, optimism, hope, mindfulness, resilience, and ultimately performance. One example of this has been highlighted in news reports and in the sports community. The Seattle Seahawks' coaching staff has added meditation and yoga to the everyday practice routine to help build resilience in the face of stress, optimism, and happiness among the players (Roenigk, 2013). These guided meditation sessions look inward and focus on visualizing the best versions of themselves, or in this case, success on the football field. Although not mandatory, more than 20 players weekly commit to these meditation and mindfulness practices with the team sport psychologist (Roenigk, 2013).

The Seahawks' approach is one anecdotal example to help illustrate a movement within the sport community for embracing the ideas behind positive psychology as valid, effective ways to help players improve. In a pilot study in Australia, a positive sport-coaching model was implemented among a group of first team football and soccer players at the high school level (Waters et al., 2011). The positive model analyzes what went well for athletes in their training and games, followed by processing and praising the past experience. Following the processing of that experience, if negative or non positive actions ensued, the coaches work to explain those with an optimistic mindset. Coaches are then charged with outlining "to-do" strategies for further growth. Last, coaches review what went well for the athlete in that particular experience again (Waters et al., 2011).

In the study by Waters et al. (2011), results included decreased nerves for the athletes, enthusiasm for learning, and an increased positive perspective for both coaches and athletes. Further research through a quasi-experimental longitudinal study is currently underway at the same school to expand upon these results with more than 50 coaches and 600 athletes (Scholes & Waters, 2012).

Helping Students Thrive as Both Leaders and Athletes. According to leadership development theory and models, the more advanced leaders understand that they always have more to learn (Komives et al., 2005), and a learning orientation can lead to higher self-efficacy as a leader (Avolio & Hannah, 2008). Therefore, as part of leadership development for students, a growth or learning mindset in all areas of the educational process is essential to success (De Castella et al., 2013; Yeager & Dweck, 2012). Additionally, self-efficacy, resilience, and engagement are important factors in developing leadership capacities (Avolio & Hannah, 2008; Csikszentmihalyi, 1990; Dugan et al., 2014). The next section explains how these important concepts of well-being connect to sport participation and athletics and how staff and faculty can help students thrive as both leaders and athletes.

Improving Self-Efficacy. Developing positive self-efficacy is also important for helping students become better leaders (Avolio & Hannah, 2008). Self-efficacy can be developed through the mastery of skills and competencies (Bandura, 1994). In recreation and sport, gaining physical strength or capacity can help students feel confident in their abilities in other areas as well (Mutrie & Faulkner, 2004). This self-efficacy can be channeled into creating additional leadership experiences for students that allow them to continue to master new skills. Perhaps the club lacrosse player who has developed a strong capacity for the sport and for his or her role on the team is ready for additional challenges as the club's treasurer. Or maybe group fitness instructors who are able to motivate large groups of fitness participants in a class can serve as the student supervisors in their area to advance these skills in expansive roles. Career counselors often recommend that students are aware of the transferable skills that they can take from collegiate experiences and explain to an employer how those are relevant to the workplace. It is essential to highlight those transferable skills, abilities, and knowledge for students while they are still on campus and help them draw those connections early on so they can use their talents and abilities in multiple arenas and across leadership experiences.

NEW DIRECTIONS FOR STUDENT LEADERSHIP • DOI: 10.1002/yd

Building Resilience.   An emphasis on resilience building creates a space for strengths-based and positive psychology principles to influence the leadership development process. In sport research, developing resilience is defined more often as developing mental toughness.

> Mental toughness is the presence of some or the entire collection of experientially developed and inherent values, attitudes, emotions, cognitions, and behaviors that influence the way in which an individual approaches, responds to, and appraises both negatively and positively construed pressures, challenges, and adversities to consistently achieve his or her goals. (Coulter, Mallett, & Gucciardi, 2010, p. 715)

The mental toughness that is encouraged by participation in sport no doubt helps students with resilience building and translates into other challenges they face with academics, work, or in their personal lives (De Castella et al., 2013; Yeager & Dweck, 2012). And as mentioned earlier in this chapter, resilience in leadership development has been shown to contribute positively to a leader's ability to cope with challenge and stress. This would be a great transferable skill for an athlete to bring to a leadership role outside of the context of sport.

Conclusion

This chapter has sought to draw connections between research and practice within positive psychology, sport psychology, and leadership studies to support positive leadership development. In practice, many of the strategies that are used to boost success are similar and grounded in research on mindfulness, happiness, optimism, and a focus on talent development. Students who pursue athletics or who engage in recreational opportunities while in school are likely to develop positive skills and competencies that can be translated to academics or future success. A team-oriented mindset, perseverance, and resilience are all possible outcomes of recreational involvement. But the development of student-athletes does not have to stop there. Incorporating elements of talent/strength development, developing a growth mindset, and developing self-efficacy are all additional outcomes that can be achieved and linked to leadership development. If coaches, administrators, and teachers incorporate a strengths-based approach to overall student development, students can learn to use their talents and maximize their potential for success in all areas of their lives.

References

Anderson, M. (2012). *The leader development of college students who participate in different levels of sport.* Unpublished doctoral dissertation, The Ohio State University,

Columbus. Retrieved from https://etd.ohiolink.edu/!etd.send_file?accession=osu1339154225&disposition=inline

Avolio, B., & Hannah, S. (2008). Developmental readiness: Accelerating leader development. *Consulting Psychology Journal, 60*, 331–347.

Bandura, A. (1994). Self-efficacy. In R. J. Corsini (Ed.), *Encyclopedia of psychology* (2nd ed., Vol. 3, pp. 368–368). New York, NY: Wiley.

Coulter, T. J., Mallett, C. J., & Gucciardi, D. F. (2010). Understanding mental toughness in Australian soccer: Perceptions of players, parents, and coaches. *Journal of Sports Sciences, 28*, 699–716.

Clifton, D. O., & Harter, J. K. (2003). Investing in strengths. In A. K. S. Cameron, B. J. E. Dutton, & C. R. E. Quinn (Eds.), *Positive organizational scholarship: Foundations of a new discipline* (pp. 111–121). San Francisco, CA: Berrett-Koehler.

Csikszentmihalyi, M. (1990). *Flow: The psychology of optimal experience*. New York, NY: HarperCollins.

De Castella, K., Goldin, P., Jazaieri, H., Ziv, M., Dweck, C. S., & Gross, J. J. (2013). Beliefs about emotion: Links to emotion regulation, well-being, and psychological distress. *Basic and Applied Social Psychology, 35*, 497–505.

Dugan, J. P., Kodama, C., Correia, B., & Associates. (2013). *Multi-Institutional Study of Leadership insight report: Leadership program delivery*. College Park, MD: National Clearinghouse for Leadership Programs.

Dugan, J. P., Torrez, M. A., & Turman, N. T. (2014). *Leadership in intramural sports and club sports: Examining influences to enhance educational impact*. Corvallis, OR: NIRSA.

Gable, S. L., & Haidt, J. (2005). What (and why) is positive psychology? *Review of General Psychology, 9*, 103–110.

Gallup, Inc. (2014). *Great jobs, great lives*: The 2014 Gallup-Purdue Index Report. Retrieved from http://www.gallup.com/file/services/176771/Gallup%20Purdue%20Index%20Flyer.pdf

Gordon, S. (2012). Strengths-based approaches to developing mental toughness: Team and individual. *International Coaching Psychology Review, 7*, 210–222.

Gould, D. (2002). Sport psychology in the new millennium: The psychology of athletic excellence and beyond. *Journal of Applied Sport Psychology, 14*, 137–139.

Harter J., & Rath, T. (2010). *Well-being: The five essential elements*. New York NY: Gallup Press.

Higher Education Research Institute [HERI]. (1996). *A social change model of leadership development: Guidebook* (Ver. III). College Park, MD: National Clearinghouse for Leadership Programs.

Komives, S. R., Lucas, N., & McMahon, T. R. (2013). *Exploring leadership: For college students who want to make a difference* (3rd ed.). San Francisco, CA: Jossey-Bass.

Komives, S. R., Owen, J. E., Longerbeam, S. D., Mainella, F. C., & Osteen, L. (2005). Developing a leadership identity: A grounded theory. *Journal of College Student Development, 46*, 593–611.

Mutrie, N., & Faulkner, G. (2004). Physical activity: Positive psychology in motion. In P. A. Linley, & S. Joseph (Eds.), *Positive psychology in practice* (pp. 146–164). Hoboken, NJ: John Wiley & Sons.

Rath, T., & Conchie, B. (2008). *Strengths-based leadership*. New York, NY: Gallup Press.

Roenigk, A. (2013). *Lotus pose on two*. Retrieved from http://espn.go.com/nfl/story/_/id/9581925/seattle-seahawks-use-unusual-techniques-practice-espn-magazine

Scholes, M., & Waters, L. (2012). Creating a positive sports organization. Presentation at the First Canadian Conference on Positive Psychology, Toronto University, Canada.

Seligman, M. E., & Csikszentmihalyi, M. (2000). Positive psychology: An introduction. *American Psychologist, 55*, 1–14.

Seligman, M. E., Steen, T. A., Park, N., & Peterson, C. (2005). Positive psychology progress: Empirical validation of interventions. *American Psychologist, 60*, 410–421.

Waters, L., Scholes, M., & White, M. (2011). *Using positive psychology to promote well-being in student athletes: A pilot evaluation at St. Peters College, Adelaide.* Poster session presented at the APS College of Educational and Developmental Psychologists National Conference, Melbourne, Australia.

Yeager, D. S., & Dweck, C. S. (2012). Mindsets that promote resilience: When students believe that personal characteristics can be developed. *Educational Psychologist, 47,* 302–314.

Amy C. Barnes *is a senior lecturer in the Higher Education and Student Affairs program at the Ohio State University. She also teaches courses in the undergraduate Leadership Studies minor.*

James Larcus *is a graduate student in the Higher Education and Student Affairs program at the Ohio State University.*

8

This chapter provides background in adventure education and its connection to student leadership pedagogy. An adventure program is the ideal experiential learning setting promoting students' leadership development through direct experience, reflection, and application.

Adventure Leadership and Experiential Education

Elizabeth A. Speelman, Mark Wagstaff

Backpacking in a remote wilderness, gliding down a giant zip line, or navigating class III whitewater may well be one of the best-kept secrets when contemplating student leadership development. Many perceive outdoor recreation as an important leisure outlet but tend not to associate participation in adventurous activities with development of socially responsible leaders. Colleges and universities across the United States boast outdoor recreation programs as an integral service for their students. Programs that are managed and facilitated by full-time, trained adventure educators provide a unique option among the myriad of programming choices for student involvement.

The purpose of this chapter is twofold. First, an emphasis is placed on demonstrating how adventure education blends with the high-impact practices in student leadership development. Specifically, outdoor adventure programs are conducive to supporting student growth through the stages of the Leadership Identity Development (LID) model mentioned in previous chapters (Komives, Longerbeam, Owen, Mainella, & Osteen, 2006). Second, an overview of the specific tools and theories used in adventure education is present and linked to the contemporary practices of student leadership development. For the purpose of this chapter, the term adventure education encompasses the broad terminology used to describe outdoor adventure-based programs within traditional academic and recreational student service offerings. Adventure education differs from a leisure service in terms of the sound pedagogy and growth-oriented facilitation methods that embody adventure education programming.

New Directions for Student Leadership, no. 147, Fall 2015 © 2015 Wiley Periodicals, Inc., A Wiley Company
Published online in Wiley Online Library (wileyonlinelibrary.com) • DOI: 10.1002/yd.20146

To provide context for those not intimately familiar with adventure education on the college campus, a brief example is provided within the framework of high-impact practices discussed in Chapter 2. The typical campus outdoor education program provides adventure-based services such as a wilderness-based trip program, climbing/bouldering wall facility, outdoor equipment rental, and challenge course/ropes course program. Some outdoor trips include a community service component such as a river cleanup or trail maintenance at the local mountain biking area. Students register for experiences led by trained peer leaders. As participants gain more confidence and experience, they sign up for advanced activities and may eventually integrate into the program as a peer leader. Peer leaders go through an intensive training regimen facilitated by full-time staff and peer trainers to develop the technical competencies and leadership skills necessary to lead. Powerful mentoring relationships are forged during the dynamic of training and intensity of trip leading. Peer leaders tend to experience a strong sense of belonging and membership when part of the staff.

From the participant standpoint, students engage in an intense, small group experience and are encouraged by peer mentors to actively participate in every aspect of the process. Participants become involved in classic group dynamics around complex decision making, navigating personal and group needs, and wrestling with individual differences. This is a powerful forum for facilitating the high-impact practices of sociocultural peer conversations and developing leadership self-efficacy through mentoring relationships. Participants tend to develop a sense of belonging and establish meaningful relationships with staff and other participants that transfer to all areas of collegiate life. Because of these experiences and exposure, students are more prone to participate in the high-impact practice of engaging in outdoor-based, off-campus groups such as the local caving club, whitewater boating group, community mountain biking team, or local search and rescue squad. To gain a better understanding of how adventure education works as a developmental process, let us review the history and theory behind adventure education.

History of Adventure Education

Adventure education programs in the United States originated from organized camp experiences such as the Boy Scouts and Girl Scouts of America (Raiola & O'Keefe, 1999). These organizations sought to develop young individuals physically and mentally to be conscientious and responsible members of society. Additionally, Outward Bound schools substantially influenced the progression of adventure education in the United States. Kurt Hahn, the founder of the Outward Bound schools in Great Britain (Priest & Gass, 2005), believed in creating dynamic experiences that allowed students the opportunity to learn about their personal abilities, gain self-confidence, and develop a sense of responsibility for others. Project Adventure, an offshoot of the Outward Bound schools, was specifically developed to integrate adventure education into schools (Prouty, 1999). Curriculum was developed to incorporate the principles of adventure education across core classes in the high school setting.

Outdoor outing clubs, which eventually evolved into contemporary outdoor recreation programming, represented the start of adventure education in universities and colleges (Watters, 1986). Today, adventure education programs in higher education take many forms. Outdoor orientation programs for first-year students facilitate student transition and preparation for college (Vlamis, Bell, & Gass, 2011). Students in residential communities engage in adventure programs to facilitate relationships with peers and faculty that lead to awareness of peer support and mentorship opportunities (Bobilya & Akey, 2002). Leadership programs on campus supplement their curricula with adventure to build confidence, create a safe environment for success and failure, and illustrate differences in leadership for their participants, among other outcomes (Merritt, 2010). Student organizations and sports teams use this opportunity to identify team leaders and build cohesion (Fletcher & Meyer, 2009). Each of these experiences provides the opportunity for individuals to apply the language and theory of leadership into a group setting where they can start to understand the skills needed to work within a team enabling them to transition in the LID model from "leader identified" to "leadership differentiated" (Komives et al., 2006).

Theory Supporting Adventure Education

Although adventure education did not result from a specific educational theory, many foundational theories and ideas support adventure education as a pedagogic practice. In particular, the theory and philosophy of experiential education plays a central role. John Dewey, one of the founders of modern experiential education (Breunig, 2008), believed that subject matter should not be learned in isolation but rather in collaboration with the local environment. Students should learn through a process that promotes the connection of experiences to future learning (Frank, 2004). David Kolb (1984) believed that the experience itself was not enough and developed the Experiential Learning Cycle. This cycle consists of four components: concrete experience, reflection, generalization, and application. After an individual has an experience, reflection provides the opportunity to create meaning from the experience. Generalization allows an individual or the group to identify patterns in behavior or connections to broader concepts. Finally, application provides an opportunity to incorporate specific learning or determine concrete changes to future experiences (Frank, 2004). The role of the facilitator in these discussions is to provide a spark to ignite a conversation, bring new knowledge to the students, and create an atmosphere conducive to open sharing. The role of the student is to share his or her perspectives, gather new information and ideas from others in the group, and respectfully challenge ideas. The result can be a new or deeper understanding of personal beliefs and values that inform leadership development.

As a developmental tool, the primary purpose of adventure education is to promote change (Luckner & Nadler, 1997). Change manifests shifts in knowledge, attitude, and skills. These shifts provide an opportunity for leadership development. The research participants associated with the LID model (Komives et al., 2006) all started college in stage three "leader identified." As participants develop mastery in adventure-based skills, they are most often under supervision and given leadership opportunities by peer mentors. In a college outdoor program, the act of peer mentorship promotes change for both the participant and the student mentor. Whereas the participant or evolving leader may still be transitioning between "leader identified" and "leadership differentiated," the student mentor is gaining insight into the "generativity" stage in which mentoring is identified as a part of their leadership identity (Komives et al., 2006).

Collegiate adventure education programs are advancing and refining their ability to support and evaluate student leadership development (Harrison & Erpelding, 2012). The theories that support adventure education align with the LID model (Komives et al., 2006) and the results of the Multi-Institutional Study of Leadership (MSL; Dugan, Kodama, Correia, & Associates, 2013). But what actually happens during the adventure education experience to facilitate growth and change? The following section provides an overview of common methods and techniques used to facilitate these programs.

Facilitating Adventure-Based Experiences

The role of the facilitator is to provide an opportunity for individuals or groups to work through an experience by taking a student-centered approach verses a leader-centered approach. Although the facilitator creates the experience with intention toward a specific outcome, it is the participants who ultimately construct meaning from the experience. The facilitator uses techniques such as the full-value contract (FVC), challenge by choice (CBC), sequencing, and processing to create a safe learning environment conducive to growth.

Full-value, or behavioral, contracts constitute agreements made between group members. Simply, they are articulated expectations around acceptable individual and group behavior (Schoel & Maizell, 2002). FVCs set the tone for healthy group norm development and the open communication necessary to fully engage in the group process. Respect, selflessness, active listening, honesty, trying one's hardest, and openness to critical feedback are examples of typical attributes found in a FVC. These contracts can be dictated by the facilitator, cocreated between the facilitator and the participants or completely created by the participants.

Adventure activities promote movement from a place of relative comfort and push students to test new ideas and practice new skills. Participants are challenged physically and mentally and may experience feelings of vulnerability or fear. The concept of CBC (Schoel, Prouty, & Radcliffe, 1988) empowers students to make decisions regarding their level of participation. Although not all aspects of the program may be a choice once started (e.g., location, weather, time of day), participants choose their level of engagement guided by the FVC. For example, a group of students from diverse backgrounds go rock climbing. The more privileged students in the group who attended summer camps and expensive outdoor schools when younger are eager to climb. Others in the group, with less privileged backgrounds, are hesitant to climb. One such student chooses not to scale an 80-foot climb but instead serves as safety belayer for other group members. This important, technical responsibility constitutes a vital group role for the day. At day's end, during the group reflection period, the student feels a sense of accomplishment as opposed to failure for opting out of the climb. During the lively discussion that evening, group members realize that reaching the top was less important and realized the power of CBC guided by the FVC. By working together the group experienced an incredible day due to genuine teamwork. The peer leader encourages the sharing of personal life stories. As a result, rich and beneficial conversations ensue around the sociocultural issues of class and privilege.

Behavioral contracts and CBC aid in setting expectations and the tone for leadership development, which is consistent with key learning outcomes in stage three, "leader identified," of the LID model (Komives et al., 2006). In addition, sequencing activities within the adventure experience further develop the educational framework for change and transition. As reported in the MSL (Dugan et al., 2013), the developmental readiness of the students must be considered and accounted for when sequencing an experience. A well-trained facilitator is experienced not only in the theoretical aspects of individual and group development but also in making ongoing assessments of the group throughout the experience. Programs achieve success when activities are planned to meet the group where they are physically, emotionally, and developmentally, with room for adaptation as needed.

In addition to the FVC, CBC, and sequencing, processing is a vital facilitation technique that relates to both the manner in which the activities are set up (framed) and how they are debriefed (Stanchfield, 2008). For some experiences, such as a staff training trip on a local river, the program director might ensure that safety aspects are firmly in place and then take a hands-off approach to leading the new staff down the river. The purpose of the trip is three fold: (a) to improve paddling skills, (b) to develop leadership decision-making skills, and (c) to complete a service project for the local land management agency. The group naturally struggles without the direct aid of the experienced leader. After the trip, the director has the student staff reflect on the experience through a structured discussion accompanied by a prepared lesson. Due to the difficulties experienced, the group is ripe to learn and absorb decision-making models and theory presented by the director. The director then assigns staff to write individual reflection papers on how they will integrate newfound knowledge into their leadership styles. Papers are then collected and discussed during one-on-one staff meetings with the director and later put into the student's leadership portfolio.

Another way to frame and process the experience is through the use of metaphors (Beames, 2012). Facilitators may create metaphors between the activity that the group is completing and the current challenges the student group may be going through in real life. For example, the student senate and elected officers are spending a day on the challenge course. The group attempts to accomplish the giant spider's web by getting the group through the holes without touching. The metaphor might be that the sticky spider's web represents navigating the complex and sticky relationships currently within the student senate. Navigating these challenging relationships is played out experientially by trying to accomplish the task followed by a structured debriefing designed to address the issues faced interpersonally within the senate. Students begin to discover that both the personal and cultural influences that individuals bring to their group matter and affect their ability to communicate effectively.

Typically at the end of an adventure activity, whether a day hike or challenge course event, the leader facilitates group processing to aid in the transfer of learning from the experience to specific real life situations. This time of structured reflection, whether individually or between participants, maximizes the educational value and developmental power of adventure programming. This is an opportunity for students to share and connect about their personal experiences, which influence their leadership beliefs. Sharing of personal social and cultural influences among peers provides students different perspectives by which they can examine their own beliefs and values. Working through differences of opinions and beliefs also lays the groundwork for students to transition to stage four of the LID model, "leadership differentiated" (Komives et al., 2006).

Models for Consideration

By this point in the chapter, it should be apparent that outdoor recreation activities alone do not facilitate leadership development. The theories and methodologies exercised in an adventure education context must be employed. The following program descriptions represent two different approaches in using adventure education to effect student leadership development.

Adventure Leadership Institute.   Oregon State University (OSU) at Corvallis founded the Adventure Leadership Institute (ALI) in 1947. This high-impact program housed in the department of OSU Recreational Sports prides itself on using "experience as the textbook and the outdoors as the classroom" ("Recreational Sports," n.d.a.). The ALI clearly publicizes that its foundational philosophies and theories, such as Kolb's Learning Theory (Kolb, 1984), Tuckman's stages of group development (Priest & Gass, 2005), and Hersey and Blanchard's Model of Situational Leadership (Hersey, Blanchard, & Johnson, 2007), drive their program design and outcomes. They intentionally develop student leadership abilities by placing them in positions to guide and facilitate outdoor adventure experiences. They use experiential learning and reflective experiences to foster problem-solving skills and self-identity. They conduct their own in-house research to assess program outcomes and use instruments like the Challenge Course Experience Questionnaire, implemented pre and posttest. ALI staff found participant growth in the areas of critical thinking, pluralism, collaboration, social responsibility, and self-awareness after participation in their challenge course program ("Recreational Sports," n.d.b).

The cornerstone of their program is an in-house certification program designed to train and assess adventure trip leaders and challenge course facilitators. Students take a series of academic courses, outdoor industry recognized certification workshops, and apprenticeship experiences to achieve the competencies needed for overall in-house certification. Through the training of professionally competent adventure leaders, the ALI is contributing to OSU student leadership development.

Georgia College Leadership Programs.   The Georgia College Leadership Programs are intended to develop student leaders within all academic disciplines ("Leadership Programs," n.d.). These programs are open to all Georgia College students and although they are not specifically adventure education programs, they do employ the use of adventure education to supplement leadership development of the students. The Emerging Leaders program, a program exclusively for Georgia College freshman, focuses on the identification of personal leadership skills and values as well as opportunities for leadership within the university and community. The Leadership Certificate Program (LCP) and the Georgia Education Mentorship (GEM) are more advanced programs focusing on the practices and principles of leadership through the study of leadership theories and models as well as hands-on leadership and mentorship opportunities ("Leadership Programs," n.d.).

All three programs supplement their curriculum with adventure education activities. The following is an example from the Emerging Leaders program. To start each academic year, new students in this program along with their peer leaders participate in teambuilding activities at the Outdoor Center at Georgia College. The main purpose of the program is for students to participate in a shared experience where they start to consider their understanding of leadership. Activities are selected to challenge students to consider the role of goal setting, group planning, and different types and styles of leadership. Students begin to develop relationships and ideas are seeded that will be cultivated during the rest of the year.

Summary. Beyond these two examples, many other models exist that facilitate the high-impact practices leading to student leadership development. A final point of discussion, no matter the programming model used, is the influence of participation in adventure education and its relationship to off-campus activities. Students who develop a passion for adventure activities are more likely to seek out additional avenues to participate and grow. The authors of this chapter have witnessed firsthand the powerful influence of meaningful participation. Students who become avid boaters, hard-core cavers, passionate mountain bikers, dedicated hikers, or advocates of Leave No Trace environmental practices seek out other avenues to pursue their newfound appetites for adventure. Not only are they seeking ways in which they can continue their own experiences but they are also finding ways to share their passion with others. As a result of on-campus participation, students have joined local search and rescue squads, regional boating clubs, local mountain biking teams, or resident environmental advocacy groups. Membership in these off campus groups represents one more high-impact practice directly correlated with student leadership development.

Conclusion

Campuses that support adventure education programming possess a powerful leadership development tool. The act of being outdoors or participating in adventure alone is not the key to growth. Campuses must intentionally develop programs led by rigorously trained professionals and student staff to facilitate experiential learning conducive to leadership development. The four high impact leadership practices identified in the MSL (Dugan et al., 2013)—(a) engaging in social-cultural conversations with peers, (b) entering into mentoring relationships, (c) community service, and (d) promoting membership in off-campus organizations—are clearly aligned with campus-based adventure education, though an increase in research that explicitly investigates these connections is warranted.

The results of a study on afterschool programs, completed by the Collaborative for Academic, Social, and Emotional Learning (CASEL; n.d.), make an appropriate summary for this chapter. CASEL (n.d.) is a national organization dedicated to the advancement of evidence-based social and emotional learning in education. They determined that programs that were SAFE (sequenced, active, focused, and explicit) were the most successful (Durlak & Weissberg, 2007). Having qualified staff implementing programs will assist in keeping students physically safe, and designing SAFE programs will enhance the opportunities for personal leadership development.

References

Beames, S. (2012). The conscious use (or avoidance) of metaphor in outdoor adventure education. *Pathways: The Ontario Journal of Outdoor Education, 24*(4), 24–27.

Bobilya, A. J., & Akey, L. D. (2002). An evaluation of adventure education components in a residential learning community. *Journal of Experiential Education, 25,* 296–304.

Breunig, M. (2008). The historical roots of experiential education. In K. Warren, D. Mitten, & T. A. Loeffler (Eds.), *Theory & practice of experiential education* (pp. 77–92). Boulder, CO: Association for Experiential Education.

Collaborative for Academic, Social, and Emotional Learning [CASEL]. (n.d.) *About CASEL.* Retrieved from http://www.casel.org/about/

Dugan, J. P., Kodama, C., Correia, B., & Associates. (2013). *Multi-institutional study of leadership insight report: Leadership program delivery.* College Park, MD: National Clearinghouse for Leadership Programs.

Durlak, J., & Weissberg, R. (2007). *The impact of after-school programs that promote personal and social skills.* Chicago, IL: Collaborative for Academic, Social, and Emotional Learning.

Fletcher, T., & Meyer, B. (2009). Cohesion and trauma: An examination of a collegiate women's volleyball team. *Journal of Humanistic Counseling, Education, and Development, 48,* 173–194.

Frank, L. (2004). *Journey toward the caring classroom.* Oklahoma City, OK: Wood 'N' Barnes Publishing & Distribution.

Harrison, G., & Erpelding, M. (2012). *Outdoor program administration: Principles and practices.* Champaign, IL: Human Kinetics.

Hersey, P., Blanchard, K., & Johnson, D. E. (2007). *Management of organizational behavior: Utilizing human resources* (7th ed.). New Jersey, NJ: Prentice Hall.

Kolb, D. A. (1984). *Experiential learning: Experience as the source of learning and development.* Englewood Cliffs, NJ: Prentice-Hall.

Komives, S., Longerbeam, S., Owen, J., Mainella, F., & Osteen, L. (2006). A leadership identity development model: Applications from a grounded theory. *Journal of College Student Development, 47,* 401–418.

Leadership Programs. (n.d.). *GC leadership programs.* Retrieved from http://www.gcsu .edu/leadership/

Luckner, J., & Nadler, R. (1997). *Processing the experience; Strategies to enhance and generalize learning.* Dubuque, IA: Kendall/Hunt Publishing Company.

Merritt, H. (2010). *Impacts of a ropes course experience on a leadership development program.* Unpublished master's thesis, California State University, Sacramento. Retrieved from http://csus-dspace.calstate.edu/bitstream/handle/10211.9/1018/HunterMerritt .pdf?sequence=1

Priest, S., & Gass, M. (2005). *Effective leadership in adventure programming* (2nd ed.). Champaign, IL: Human Kinetics.

Prouty, D. (1999). Project Adventure: A brief history. In J. C. Miles & S. Priest (Eds.), *Adventure programming* (pp. 93–101). State College, PA: Venture Publishing.

Raiola, E., & O'Keefe, M. (1999). Philosophy in practice: A history of adventure programming. In J. C. Miles & S. Priest (Eds.), *Adventure programming* (pp. 93–101). State College, PA: Venture Publishing.

Recreational Sports. (n.d.a). *Theories, values, and foundations.* Retrieved from http:// oregonstate.edu/recsports/ALI/theories-values-and-foundations

Recreational Sports. (n.d.b). *ALI™ Research.* Retrieved from http://recsports.oregonstate .edu/ali/ali-research

Schoel, J., & Maizell, R. (2002). *Exploring islands of healing: New perspectives on adventure-based counseling.* Dubuque, IA: Kendall Hunt.

Schoel, J., Prouty, D., & Radcliffe, P. (1988). *Islands of healing: A guide to adventure- based counseling.* Dubuque, IA: Kendall Hunt.

Stanchfield, J. (2008). *Tips and tools: The art of experiential group facilitation.* Oklahoma City, OK: Wood 'N' Barnes Publishing & Distribution.

Vlamis, E., Bell, B., & Gass, M. (2011). The first year effects of an adventure orientation program on the student development behaviors of incoming college students. *Journal of Experiential Education, 34,* 127–148.

Watters, R. (1986). *Outdoor program handbook.* Pocatello, ID: Idaho State University Press.

ELIZABETH A. SPEELMAN *is a lecturer in outdoor education in the School of Health and Human Performance at Georgia College.*

MARK WAGSTAFF *is a professor in the Department of Recreation, Parks, and Tourism at Radford University.*

9

This chapter provides the reader with literature and resources for conducting leadership assessment in collegiate recreation and athletics. Current practices and strategies are shared.

Leadership Assessment in Collegiate Recreation and Athletics

Sarah E. Hardin

As the focus on leadership development within collegiate curricular and cocurricular opportunities has grown in recent years, so has the need to determine outcomes of those opportunities. Institutions have had to create and improve upon assessment strategies and appropriate tools for measuring leadership development. The effectiveness of intentional leadership development practices within any program or cocurricular offering is dependent upon appropriate assessment of the impact and outcomes of those intentional practices. This chapter identifies more prominent methodologies and instruments that have been used to assess various aspects of leadership. Current practices in leadership programs and assessment within collegiate athletics and recreation are also discussed. Finally, important considerations in the construction of a leadership development assessment strategy are identified.

Leadership Development Assessment Methodologies

As Adam Goodman (2013) notes, there is a compelling argument to be made that if program staff members and faculty are serious about leadership development, they should also be serious about assessment. John Schuh and Associates (2009) refer to assessment as an "essential dimension of contemporary student affairs practice" (p. 1). The primary rationale for administrators to collect data on student learning and developmental outcomes related to collegiate experiences includes, among other things, (a) establishing accountability for cocurricular activities; (b) reporting cocurricular contributions to student learning; and (c) providing information critical to organizational effectiveness and strategic planning. Additionally, assessment can

New Directions for Student Leadership, no. 147, Fall 2015 © 2015 Wiley Periodicals, Inc., A Wiley Company
Published online in Wiley Online Library (wileyonlinelibrary.com) • DOI: 10.1002/yd.20147

lead to improved student self-awareness, goal setting, and commitment to development (Boatman, 2000).

Previously in this publication, the reader has seen the classification of the term leadership in varying perspectives: as a character trait, set of skills or competencies, a system of behavior, a process of development, or characteristics developed through formal positions or roles. Whereas assessment of intangible characteristics is always difficult, leadership is especially challenging due to its many facets. Difficulty in finding a common definition and consensus on the observable leadership behaviors has led to a scarcity of research into the outcome of leadership development within the collegiate environment.

The interpretation of the defining elements of leadership development and the practitioner or researcher perspective should be the greatest determining factor in the type of instrument and methodology used in a specific assessment project. As theories and models have been developed in an attempt to explain the facets of leadership, so have tools and instruments in an attempt to operationalize them. This chapter primarily focuses on literature and instruments related to the functions of assessing leadership behaviors and learning outcomes. Several of the most prominent of these are discussed in the sections that follow.

Competency-Based Approaches. The use of competencies to gauge student leadership as well as other developmental collegiate experiences has become very popular in the past 15 years (Komives, Lucas, & McMahon, 2013). This is based upon the belief that certain knowledge, abilities, and behaviors are foundational to an individual's development as a leader. However, because there is no set list of abilities or behaviors that can reflect all leadership perspectives, there is no consensus on one method or instrument of measurement.

One of the first validated instruments designed specifically for exploration of leadership behaviors in college students is the Student Leadership Practices Inventory (Student LPI), developed by Kouzes and Posner (1998). Behaviors that are common to successful leaders are categorized into five leadership practices (Posner, 2004) and the LPI guides the assessment of an intentional mastery of practices. On the road to validation, the Student LPI was used, among other studies, to examine leadership practices of students in campus positions of responsibility (Posner & Brodsky, 1992), as well as to explore students' progress in leadership practices when they are involved in leadership roles beyond a 1-year leadership assignment (Posner & Rosenberger, 1997). Pre- and posttests around the application of a particular intervention or experience are used to apply this instrument in longitudinal studies.

A key aspect of the Student LPI is that it has two forms of assessment: Self and Observer. Each form is used to assess the subject's identification with the five leadership practices; the Self form is completed by the student leader, whereas the Observer form is completed by individuals who are familiar with or have directly observed the behaviors of the student leader (Posner, 2004). Including the two perspectives within the assessment allows for some validation of the data that are collected on student's leadership abilities. The Student LPI has been further modified to include an assessment of self-efficacy, the belief in one's ability to engage in leadership behaviors.

In 1998, the Council for the Advancement of Standards in Higher Education (CAS; 2012) first published standards for collegiate student leadership programs. It contained provisions related to the advancement of student competencies in several categories including "foundations of leadership" (CAS, 2012). In 2009, the National Association for Campus Activities (NACA) used the CAS Standards and the Social Change Model of Leadership Development (HERI, 1996) to create *A Competency Guide for College Student Leaders* (NACA, 2009).

The competency guide is targeted toward students involved in campus leadership activities and is designed to "serve[s] as a learning map for student leaders as they grow and develop through participation" (NACA, 2009, p. 1). Student leaders are provided with a list of learning outcomes in 10 core competency areas targeted for potential achievement; however, the competency approach is also combined with the perspective that leadership is also a process that is assisted through the suggested initiatives and key questions within the guide (NACA, 2009). A facilitator's version of the guide allows for student competency self-assessment to be reviewed by a staff advisor for accuracy and feedback. Although perhaps not a validated assessment instrument for research data collection, the competency guide is a useful tool for administrators who work with student leaders in their continued development as well as to report the impact of activities on student leader self-assessed skills and observed behaviors. It encourages students not only to assess their progress toward desirable leadership competencies but to use the competency listings as aspirational guides in a developmental process.

Using the standards outlined by CAS (2012) along with components of foundational leadership models, Seemiller (2013) incorporates 60 leadership competencies within eight categories into a collegiate guidebook for intentional learning. The guidebook links specific leadership competencies to career aspirations, allowing students to seek out appropriate skills necessary for job preparation. Additional tools within the guidebook assist the student in self-evaluation and the practitioner in the design and assessment of learning experiences associated with each competency. In her approach to leadership development, Seemiller (2013) views competencies as behaviors that are indicators of learning outcomes. Students may use the guidebook to master competencies associated desired learning outcomes. Although competencies are foundational to this approach, the additional tools provide a process-oriented component.

Process-Oriented Approaches.   As more formalized positional leader training programs have emerged within higher education since the mid-1990s (Dugan & Komives, 2007), much of the exploration on student leadership development has been conducted in studies using students already active in leadership-related pursuits (Thompson, 2006). Many use studies of students within positional roles and focus on the developmental process as they progress within those roles. Goodman (2013) cautions against "trying to provide a definitive list of leadership behaviors and qualities as well as specific instructions for what [students] should do to become better leaders" (p. 7). He supports the effectiveness of a process-oriented approach that assists students in understanding of how their own behaviors and attitudes may translate into effective leadership behaviors.

In their development of the Leadership Process Theory, Allen, Stelzner, and Wielkewicz (1998) also question the competency-based models of leadership. They assert that to be effective, leadership must allow for adaptation and the ability to adjust to quickly changing global markets and expanding technological and scientific understandings (Allen et al., 1998). To explore perceptions of all students rather than simply those in positions of responsibility and view their preferences related to two opposing ways of viewing leadership, Wielkiewicz (2000) developed the Leadership Attitudes and Beliefs Scale III (LABS-III). Students are assessed on their views of leadership on the two dimensions of hierarchical or systems perspectives.

The Social Change Model of Leadership Development (SCM) in which leadership is a dynamic, evolving process with positive social change as the goal was also developed in response to theories and models that suggested leadership is a set of traits or behaviors (HERI, 1996). The SCM was operationalized by Tracy Tyree (1998) into the Socially Responsible Leadership Scale (SRLS), an instrument composed of eight separate scales, each of which measures one of the key values. Although the SRLS was not originally used widely within higher education research, it served as the basis for the instrument developed for the ongoing Multi-Institutional Study of Leadership (Dugan & Komives, 2007). Students can complete this instrument for use in leadership education programs from the website of the National Clearinghouse of Leadership Programs (www.nclp.umd.edu). A rubric for each of the eight "C"s of the SCM is included in the second edition of Leadership for a Better World: Understanding the Social Change Model of Leadership Development (Komives & Wagner, in press).

As discussed in Chapter 2, the Multi-Institutional Study of Leadership (MSL) provides a central data set that allows researchers to explore leadership outcomes, as well as the types of student experiences that produce those outcomes. With data from over 300,000 students on over 300 college campuses, the study affords researchers and practitioners alike the ability to examine the data set from unique perspectives with broad application possibilities. Already, studies based upon the MSL 2006, 2009, and 2012 have provided interesting and applicable conclusions for administrators in a variety of cocurricular activity areas on campus, including collegiate recreation (Anderson, 2012; Dugan, Torrez, & Turman, 2014; Owen, 2011).

Qualitative Approaches.   Another categorical approach to gaining information about leadership development is through qualitative exploration. Organizations and individuals who are seeking in-depth information regarding experiences and/or insight into the developmental process may find qualitative methodologies useful alone or in combination with other methodologies. Methods such as case studies, document analysis, observation, guided discussion, portfolios, and focus group and/or individual interviews are used to delve into questions that may be difficult to explore through the use of quantitative methods. For example, focus group interviews allow a researcher to ask follow-up questions to student responses in a way that survey research does not allow. A case study in which an observer is viewing student responses to real-life events can provide a wealth and depth of information about the developmental process.

A number of studies using qualitative collection methods are reported in the following sections; an example of the insight and multiple uses of such data is found in Haines (2010) study of student participation in a club sport basketball tournament: "From participating in the NCCS basketball championships I was able to become a much better leader. I also was able to see the better part of sportsmanship" (p. 12). There are multiple potential uses of this type of statement. It informs organizers as to the developmental aspects of their event, provides outcomes information regarding event participation, and additionally, has the potential to serve as a marketing tool for future involvement.

Assessment of Leadership Development in Recreation and Athletics

The modern collegiate recreation department is composed of many experiential areas including, among others, participation in programming such as aquatics, fitness and wellness activities, special events, team challenge, outdoor pursuits, intramural sports, and club sports. In addition, collegiate recreation departments are frequently one of the largest employers of student employees on college campuses, a student experience that is frequently designed to provide developmental opportunities including that of leadership and behaviors associated with leadership.

A variety of experiences are also found within the scope of intercollegiate athletics. Whereas much of its focus remains on the experience of the collegiate student-athlete, this segment of the college experience involves many subcategories of that experience, including variations among participation in revenue versus nonrevenue producing sports, Division I versus Division III programs, and team captains versus the red-shirted freshmen. Similarly to collegiate recreation, intercollegiate athletics departments are also dependent upon students who participate as student employees, involved in the administration of programs and facilities, and who take part in significantly different experiences than their program participant counterparts. Additional complexities within the student experience appear when taking into account that a number of students are significantly involved both as a program or facility participant and as employee or student leader.

Because of the varying activities within these unique areas of the campus experience, it is somewhat misleading to try to place them together into one category or even to pool all of the experiences within one of them into one study. However, much of the early literature and multi-institutional exploration of the outcomes of the student experience does just that (Astin, 1997; Pascarella & Terenzini, 2005). It is only more recently that selected research studies have treated athletics and recreation as separate entities, although there is still little delineation of subcategories of participation within them. The breakdown into subcategories is typically accomplished in smaller scale investigations that may only be conducted on one campus at a time or, as exemplified in the recent NIRSA-commissioned study of club sport and intramural athletes, through the use of the Multi-Institutional Data Set (Dugan et al., 2014). Exploration of the leadership development literature within athletics and recreation reveals the variety of student experiences both within and between these areas of the college experience.

Collegiate Athletics. Although coaches at all levels have generally asserted the positive influence of athletic participation on leadership development, there are few studies that include this question as a primary focus. In fact, much of the assessment research related to leadership within the athletics community has focused less on the development of leadership behaviors and characteristics in student-athletes and more upon coaches' leadership styles (Beam 2001; Sullivan & Kent, 2003). Another large focus of the literature regarding student-athletes is understandably related to academic performance (Pascarella, Bohr, Nora, & Terenzini, 1995; Richard & Aries, 1999; Simons, Van Rheenen, & Covington, 1999).

Of the studies solely focusing on exploring the impact of athletic participation on leadership, most include information collected from former athletes reflecting on their experiences. Early assessments within athletic programs focused on assessment of satisfaction as categorized by Schuh and Associates (2009). Ryan's (1989) survey of freshman intercollegiate athletes found a high level of satisfaction with their development of leadership abilities. Pascarella and Smart's (1991) findings were consistent with Ryan's in comparing satisfaction levels of African-American and Caucasian athletes and nonathletes 9 years after their initial enrollment in college.

In a more recent study, Dupuis, Bloom, and Loughead (2006) used semistructured interviews of former university team captains to conclude that leadership components such as interpersonal characteristics, verbal interactions, and task behaviors were developed through the process of serving as team captain. However, a study exploring leadership development through the use of validated assessment center exercises found no association between the number of season of sports team participation and level of leadership skill (Extejt & Smith, 2009).

Currently, the National Collegiate Athletic Association (NCAA) is involved in providing NCAA-member institutions with a variety of leadership programming opportunities. Leadership development consortia are conducted each year to which institutions may send student leaders. Within many of these consortia, students explore their leadership styles and those of others through the DiSC Leadership Assessment (NCAA, 2014). Results of these assessments are used to assist students in understanding individual strengths and leadership style tendencies and using this information to improve their ability to work with those of varying styles and "effectively advance... personal and career growth" (NCAA, 2014, p. 1). This undoubtedly provides valuable insight for the involved students but does not necessarily impact the assessment literature.

Collegiate Recreation.   Several studies have found a link between leadership skills and participation in collegiate recreation programs (Bryant, Banta, & Bradley, 1995; Downs & Downs, 2003; Haines, 2001). A constructive case study approach was used by Hall, Forrester, and Borsz (2008) in examining leadership development through campus recreational sports. Recreational student organization volunteer leaders were asked to respond to a case study situation and were then interviewed regarding their perspectives on the situation presented. Document analysis of their organizations, including such materials as constitutions, job descriptions, and websites, was examined to enhance interviews and provide information on student perspectives. Themes of leadership skill development that emerged from the study included, among others, organizing and planning, serving as a mentor or role model, understanding diversity, giving and receiving feedback, and problem solving/decision making (Hall et al. 2008).

Using the MSL 2006 data set, Anderson (2012) explored Leadership Self-Efficacy and Socially Responsible Leadership values across the various levels of collegiate sport team involvement, including intramurals, club, and intercollegiate athletics. Her study concluded that being involved in sport participation at any level, even controlling for precollegiate experience, did have a positive impact on self-efficacy and values related to leadership.

In a study commissioned by NIRSA and using the MSL 2012 data set, Dugan et al. (2014) examined leadership development themes among college students participating in intramural and club sport experiences. Students involved in one or both of these recreation experiences demonstrated higher leadership capacity and efficacy than those who were not involved at all. Recommendations include expanded developmental offerings for students, the intentional encouragement of students who are less confident and motivated than their peers, the promotion of peer mentoring, the provision of more sociocultural conversations surrounding participation, and avoidance of reliance on positional leadership (Dugan et al., 2014). Due to its attraction to a large percentage of students, collegiate recreation should be "viewed [by higher education institutions] as a potent vehicle through which to target learning opportunities" (Dugan et al., 2014, p. 11). Results also indicate a need for in-depth exploration of intramural and club sports as separate entities.

Conclusion

As the information in this chapter indicates, documenting student learning and development within the broad context of leadership is a complex task. There are many decisions and perspectives that must be taken into account in creating an effective assessment plan that will move a program, department, and/or institution forward in providing appropriate interventions for college students. The approach toward leadership development within higher education institutions has evolved greatly within the past 20 years and the creation of the multi-institutional data set has already had and will continue to have a great impact on the field in the future. Practitioners should plan their interventions and assessment projects with the MSL and its preliminary findings in mind. This will provide collegiate recreation and athletics departments an entry into the world of higher education and leadership to which they were not previously admitted. The results will assist practitioners in the fields of recreation and athletics to successfully and effectively influence the leadership development of student participants and employees.

References

Allen, K. E., Stelzner, S. P., & Wielkiewicz, R. M. (1998). The ecology of leadership: Adapting to the challenges of a changing world. *Journal of Leadership Studies*, 5(2), 62–82.

Anderson, M. (2012). *The leader development of college students who participate in different levels of sport.* Unpublished doctoral dissertation, The Ohio State University, Columbus. Retrieved from https://etd.ohiolink.edu/!etd.send_file?accession=osu1339154225&disposition=inline

Astin, A. W. (1997). *Four critical years: Effect of college on beliefs, attitudes, and knowledge.* San Francisco, CA: Jossey-Bass.

Beam, J. W. (2001). *Preferred leadership of NCAA Division I and II intercollegiate student-Athletes.* Unpublished doctoral dissertation, University of North Florida, Jacksonville. Retrieved from http://digitalcommons.unf.edu/etd/166

Boatman, S. A. (2000). Assessment of leadership programs: Enhancing student leadership development. *Concepts & Connections*, 9(1), 5–8.

Bryant, J., Banta, T., & Bradley, J. (1995). Assessment provides insight into the impact and effectiveness of campus recreation programs. *NASPA Journal*, 32, 153–160.

Council for Advancement of Standards in Higher Education [CAS]. (2012). Student Leadership Programs. In *CAS professional standards for higher education* (8th ed., pp. 447–457). Washington, D.C.: Author.

Downs, P. E., & Downs, K. (2003). Value of recreational sports on college campuses. *Recreational Sports Journal*, 27(1), 5–64.

Dugan, J. P., & Komives, S. R. (2007). *Developing leadership capacity in college students.* College Park, MD: National Clearinghouse for Leadership Programs.

Dugan, J. P., Torrez, M. A., & Turman, N. T. (2014). *Leadership in intramural sports and club sports: Examining influences to enhance educational impact.* Corvallis, OR: NIRSA.

Dupuis, M., Bloom, G. A., & Loughead, T. M. (2006). Team captains' perceptions of athletic leadership. *Journal of Sport Behavior, 29*(1), 60–78.

Extejt, M. M., & Smith, J. E. (2009). Leadership development through sports team participation. *Journal of Leadership Education, 8*(2), 224–237.

Goodman, A. (2013). Learning by design: Rethinking leadership competencies. *Concepts & Connections, 20*(1), 7–10.

Haines, D. J. (2001). Undergraduate student benefits from university recreation. *NIRSA Journal, 25*(1), 25–33.

Haines, D. J. (2010). *Measurement of outcomes from participation in the NIRSA NCCS Regional & National Basketball Championship.* Retrieved from http://www.nirsa.org/docs/Discover/Research/2010_Outcomes_Basketball.pdf

Hall, S. L., Forrester, S., & Borsz, M. (2008). A constructivist case study examining the leadership development of undergraduate students in campus recreational sports. *Journal of College Student Development, 49,* 125–140.

Higher Education Research Institute [HERI]. (1996). *A social change model of leadership development* (Ver. III). Los Angeles, CA: UCLA, Higher Education Research Institute.

Komives, S. R., Lucas, N., & McMahon, T. R. (2013). *Exploring leadership: For college students who want to make a difference.* San Francisco, CA: Jossey-Bass.

Komives, S. R., & Wagner, W. (Eds). (in press). *Leadership for a better world: Understanding the social change model of leadership development* (2nd ed.). San Francisco, CA: Jossey-Bass.

Kouzes. J., & Posner, B. (1998). *Student leadership practices inventory.* San Francisco, CA: Jossey-Bass.

National Association for Campus Activities (NACA). (2009). *Competency guide for college student leaders—Facilitator's version.* Columbia, SC: NACA. Retrieved from http://sbctc.edu/College/studentsvcs/naca_college_student_leader_competency_guide-facilitator_version.pdf

National Collegiate Athletic Association [NCAA]. (2014). *Leadership development program.* Retrieved from http://www.ncaa.org/about/resources/leadership-development-programs-and-resources/student-athlete-leadership-forum

Owen, J. E. (2011). Assessment and evaluation. In S. Komives, J. P. Dugan., J. E. Owen, C. Slack, W. Wagner, & Associates, *The handbook for student leadership development* (2nd ed.). San Francisco, CA: Jossey-Bass.

Pascarella, E. T., Bohr, L., Nora, A., & Terenzini, P. T. (1995). Intercollegiate athletic participation and freshman-year cognitive outcomes. *Journal of Higher Education, 66,* 369–387.

Pascarella, E. T., & Smart, J. C. (1991). Impact of intercollegiate athletic participation for African American and Caucasian men: Some further evidence. *Journal of College Student Development, 32,* 123–130.

Pascarella, E. T., & Terenzini, P. T. (2005). *How college affects students: A third decade of research* (Vol. 2). San Francisco, CA: Jossey-Bass.

Posner, B. Z. (2004). A leadership development instrument for students: Updated. *Journal of College Student Development, 45,* 443–456.

Posner, B. Z., & Brodsky, B. (1992). A leadership development instrument for college students. *Journal of College Student Development, 33,* 231–237.

Posner, B. Z., & Rosenberger, J. (1997). Effective orientation advisors are leaders too. *NASPA Journal, 35,* 46–56.

Richard, S., & Aries, E. (1999). The division III student-athlete: Academic performance, campus involvement, and growth. *Journal of College Student Development, 40,* 211–218.

NEW DIRECTIONS FOR STUDENT LEADERSHIP • DOI: 10.1002/yd

Ryan, F. J. (1989). Participation in intercollegiate athletics: Affective outcomes. *Journal of College Student Development, 30,* 122–128.

Schuh, J. H., & Associates. (2009). *Assessment methods for student affairs.* San Francisco, CA: Jossey-Bass.

Seemiller, C. (2013). *The student leadership competencies guidebook: Designing intentional leadership learning and development.* San Francisco, CA: Jossey-Bass.

Simons, H. D., Van Rheenen, D., & Covington, M. V. (1999). Academic motivation and the student athlete. *Journal of College Student Development, 40,* 151–162.

Sullivan, P. J., & Kent, A. (2003). Coaching efficacy as a predictor of leadership style in intercollegiate athletics. *Journal of Applied Sport Psychology, 15,* 1–11.

Thompson, M. D. (2006). Student leadership process development: An assessment of contributing college resources. *Journal of College Student Development, 47,* 343–350.

Tyree, T. M. (1998). *Designing an instrument to measure socially responsible leadership using the social change model of leadership development.* Unpublished doctoral dissertation, University of Maryland, College Park.

Wielkiewicz, R. M. (2000). The Leadership Attitudes and Beliefs Scale: An instrument for evaluating college students' thinking about leadership and organizations. *Journal of College Student Development, 41,* 335–347.

SARAH E. HARDIN is the associate director of campus recreation for Centers, LLC at DePaul University.

Index

NEW DIRECTIONS FOR STUDENT LEADERSHIP
ORDER FORM SUBSCRIPTION AND SINGLE ISSUES

DISCOUNTED BACK ISSUES:

Use this form to receive 20% off all back issues of *New Directions for Student Leadership*.
All single issues priced at **$23.20** (normally $29.00)

TITLE	ISSUE NO.	ISBN
_____	_____	_____
_____	_____	_____
_____	_____	_____

Call 1-800-835-6770 or see mailing instructions below. When calling, mention the promotional code JBNND to receive your discount.

SUBSCRIPTIONS: (1 YEAR, 4 ISSUES)

☐ New Order ☐ Renewal

U.S.	☐ Individual: $89	☐ Institutional: $342
CANADA/MEXICO	☐ Individual: $89	☐ Institutional: $382
ALL OTHERS	☐ Individual: $113	☐ Institutional: $416

Call 1-800-835-6770 or see mailing and pricing instructions below.
Online subscriptions are available at www.onlinelibrary.wiley.com

ORDER TOTALS:

Issue / Subscription Amount: $ _____

Shipping Amount: $ _____
(for single issues only – subscription prices include shipping)

Total Amount: $ _____

SHIPPING CHARGES:

First Item	$6.00
Each Add'l Item	$2.00

(No sales tax for U.S. subscriptions. Canadian residents, add GST for subscription orders. Individual rate subscriptions must be paid by personal check or credit card. Individual rate subscriptions may not be resold as library copies.)

BILLING & SHIPPING INFORMATION:

☐ **PAYMENT ENCLOSED:** *(U.S. check or money order only. All payments must be in U.S. dollars.)*

☐ **CREDIT CARD:** ☐ VISA ☐ MC ☐ AMEX

Card number _____Exp. Date_____

Card Holder Name_____Card Issue #_____

Signature _____Day Phone_____

☐ **BILL ME:** *(U.S. institutional orders only. Purchase order required.)*

Purchase order # _____
Federal Tax ID 13559302 • GST 89102-8052

Name_____

Address_____

Phone_____ E-mail_____

Copy or detach page and send to: **John Wiley & Sons, One Montgomery Street, Suite 1000, San Francisco, CA 94104-4594**

Order Form can also be faxed to: **888-481-2665**

PROMO JBNND